Transformational Love

Learning to Love Like Christ

AJ Silva

Sermon To Book
www.sermontobook.com

Transformational Love / AJ Silva
ISBN-13: 978-1-945793-12-7
ISBN-10: 1-945793-12-0

To my wife, Hope—you are truly an amazing creation and servant of our Almighty God. Thank you for loving me the way that you do. I love you and daily strive to love you the way Jesus loves you.

To my mother and father—thank you for showing me what love really looks like ... even when it had to be tough love. I love you both with all my heart.

CONTENTS

Foreword by Rev. Timothy R. Gaines

If you're going to follow Jesus, love is bound to become the center of your existence. It will be love that you encounter in His words, and love will be that which shapes you to be more like the One you are following. Love will summon you, draw you in, and eventually turn you into the kind of person you were created to be. To hear the calling of Jesus is to come to know what it means to be loved, and to walk in His way is to learn how to love others with all we are. While all of this is deeply and profoundly *good*, none of it is easy.

That's why I'm glad AJ Silva has taken the time to offer this collection of challenging reflections on what a life centered on love looks like, and how one goes about following Jesus to the point that love moves to the middle of life. In these pages, you'll find an engaging confluence of pastoral wisdom and insightful teaching—the kind of thing that will be helpful to those who have been following Jesus for decades, those who are just beginning to explore what it means to follow Him, and those somewhere in between.

Wherever you're coming from, this is the kind of book that will shape you to the degree that you allow. My recommendation is to read it with an open heart and embark on this journey with courage. If you'll let it, this will be a journey into the beautiful mysteries of divine love; and because it's the love of God, you'll discover a love that is boundless. May you come to know the depths of that love and to be overtaken by its goodness—and may you be changed forever along the way.

Rev. Timothy R. Gaines, Ph.D.
Asst. Professor of Religion
Trevecca Nazarene University
Nashville, TN

INTRODUCTION

Love in Context

The concept of God's love is woven throughout the pages of the Bible. However, it's impossible to understand God's love if you assume it's comparable to love as a human emotion. Such an assumption minimizes this central aspect of God's character to the extent that a person may believe He loves or does not love them depending on how they feel one day to the next. This is an error. We can never understand God's love if we begin with our own perspective—instead, we must turn to the Author of Love to truly understand how He loves.

To understand in English what kind of love the Bible is referencing, context must be considered. Take, for example, the word 'trunk.' 'Trunk' can mean the trunk of an elephant, the trunk of a car, the trunk of a tree, or the main part of the human body. It can even mean a large piece of sturdy luggage, or a superstructure over a ship's hatches—the part of the cabin of a boat that projects out over the poop deck.

6 · AJ SILVA

The only way to know what kind of trunk is being talked about in text or speech is to consider context. "Tom touched the trunk" doesn't indicate what kind of trunk is being talking about. However, the sentence "Tom excitedly reached out and put his hand through the gap in the fence to touch the gigantic grey animal's trunk" does.

Aha! It's an *elephant's* trunk!

Now we understand what's being talked about. Context illuminates much in conversation so that we don't have to assume what is being talked about. Without context, English words can mean many things.

In the same way, context is very important in understanding what God means when He says He loves us.

Taking verses out of context opens up the possibility of misinterpreting Scripture and can lead to a misunderstanding of what a particular passage is actually saying. Clarifying context will help believers and students of the Bible come to a correct understanding of what biblical love is—and what it means when God calls those He loves to love Him, and others, in return.

This kind of love is quite different from the love human beings speak of. People tend to have preset concepts about what God's love is and what it looks like because they associate it with a human, feelings-focused, emotional type of love. Human love fails; human love hurts. The secular world has crafted an idea of love that is pulling further away and is a dim shadow of God's true, perfect love. It is God's love that transcends human understanding.

A Note about the Workbook

Following each main chapter of this book, you will find a workbook section that includes reflective questions, application-oriented "action steps," and pages for recording notes. The workbook sections may prove useful for independent reflection, group study, or simply discussion with a friend, as you begin to apply critical truths about God's love to your own life and relationships in life-changing ways.

Now, join me on a journey of discovering what it means to love—and be loved—as God loves!

CHAPTER ONE

The Highest Form of Love

All you need is love, love / Love is all you need. **— John Lennon**[1]

John Lennon's song "All You Need is Love" was born from a request to bring a song to the world that would be understood by all nations—a message of love and peace. Love is all a person or a nation needs, but is the kind of love Lennon was singing about truly able to bring peace to a broken world?

Everyone wants to be loved. It's a deep-rooted longing no person can deny. But often, the love people think they want is not the kind of love they truly want or need.

When most people think of what it means to love, they immediately think of a feeling—something that makes a person happy all the time. For a moment, consider the following ways in which we as twenty-first-century Americans authoritatively speak about love: In an article in the *Huffington Post* on July 16, 2015, author Carly

Spindel wrote, "Love is a feeling of deep affection. It's an intense attachment to someone. Love draws you to that person, in ways you can't always explain."[2] Even Merriam-Webster's dictionary defines love first as a feeling of "strong affection" for a person or as "attraction based on sexual desire."[3]

It is critical that the definition of godly love not be according to human standards!

When Jesus was asked what the greatest commandment was in all of biblical law, He responded, "'Love the Lord your God with all your heart and with all your soul and with all your mind.' This is the first and greatest commandment. And the second is like it: 'Love your neighbor as yourself'" (Matthew 22:37–39 NIV). Jesus' desire for believers was that they would love as God loves. If the greatest of all commandments is to love God and to love others, we'd better know what *godly* love means!

Biblical Love

Edgar Allan Poe once wrote, "We loved with a love that was more than love."[4] Although that may seem magical and romantic, at its core this statement really doesn't make sense. "We loved with a love that is more than love"? If a person loves with something that is *more* than love, what did they express in the first place? A strong *like*?

A person might say, "I'm an expert on the subject of love," simply because they've experienced some form of love. They then take their experience and define love for everyone according to that encounter—"it must be the same for everyone! This is what love 'looks' like for all!"

In other words, love is truly in the eye of the beholder; it is whatever the person wants it to be. Unfortunately, people bring these personal definitions with them when interpreting Scripture—their own authoritative thoughts become truth when they turn to God's Word. So, for example, when they read God's Word, which says to love one another, they immediately want to say, "Yeah, sure, I love other people!"—but within *their* context and definition of the word 'love.' However, God's definition of love is beyond a Westernized, superficial meaning of "intensely liking someone."

I have been a part of the church for a long time—ever since I was very young. I've been in and out of different congregations. Over the years I've heard people profess, "I came to this congregation and started attending because this church is such a *loving* church." However, in those same congregations, people leave the church because they say the church is so *unloving*. The error is that love becomes defined within the eye of the beholder. The individual gets to pick and choose what love looks like. I believe this is one of the top reasons people leave their churches.

In the English language, the word 'love' is vague and quite ambiguous. For instance, I cannot say that my love for my wife is the same as my love for pizza. At least I would hope that wasn't the case, right? Well, love for a spouse and love for pizza just isn't the same. But in the English language all we have is that word to go by—

love—and we have to rely heavily on context for how to frame that word.

In English, people may say, "I love this," or "I love that," identifying love according to what each has decided it means to them. Is love always romantic, or sexual? Or does it simply mean an intense "like"? The result is a pile of definitions as vast as sand on a seashore because every person on the planet brings with their definition a different perspective or worldly idea of what love means.

Unfortunately, people bring with them their own definition of what they think love is, and for them it becomes truth—equal to the Word of God.

Scripture was not originally written in English. There are actually a variety of words, with their own denotations and connotations, which have all been translated into the English word 'love.' To better understand a passage or word in Scripture, it's important to consider the original language each passage was written in—either Hebrew or Greek (or Aramaic, in which a small portion of Scripture was written, in the books of Daniel and Revelation). This is vital, too, in understanding what it means that God "loves," and that He calls us to "love" as He loves.

It doesn't matter what the most beloved authors write about love, or even what I say love is. What matters is what the authoritative Word of God says, and it is the only way to understand what God's biblical love looks like and what He means when He says He calls His children to love. Love cannot be defined by human understanding; this unique, very other-worldly and divine love can only be defined by God.

Godly love is quite different from human love.

Biblical Meanings of Love

The New Testament authors wrote, for the most part, in Koine Greek. In Greek, there are at least four main thoughts regarding love, and thus four main words that express not just any love but specific *types* of love.[5] Understanding these words sheds storehouses of light on what God means when He says He loves us and when He commands us to love others! Let's consider those different meanings, which will provide a solid foundation moving forward.

Eros

The first kind of love in Greek culture is *eros* love. From this Greek word, the English word 'erotic' is derived—which indicates exactly what kind of love this is! *Eros* is the Greek word used to communicate sexual love, or emotions connected with arousal.[6] *Eros* is a romantic type of love—a love that would be expressed toward a significant other. It is something that draws two people passionately and physically to each other. However, *eros* is not used at all in the New Testament.

Storgē

Another kind of love in Greek culture is *storgē*. *Storgē* is a familial type of love, the love that a parent has for a child: "cherishing one's kindred, especially parents or children; the mutual love of parents and children and wives and husbands; loving affection; prone to love;

loving tenderly; chiefly of the reciprocal tenderness of parents and children."[7] It is the adoring bond that exists between mothers, fathers, sons, daughters, sisters and brothers. It's a good, beautiful, and natural love. Like *eros, storgē* is not found in the Bible.

Phileo

Next, let's look at *phileo*, a verb that is found in the New Testament. *Phileo* love is related to the Greek nouns *philia* and *philadelphia*, as in the American "city of brotherly love." The *phileo* kind of love is brotherly love, as found between close friends who reciprocate affection. *Strong's Concordance* defines this kind of love as "the love which Christians cherish for each other as brethren."[8]

Paul wrote about *phileo* love, exhorting believers to "love one another with mutual affection [*philadelphia*]; outdo one another in showing honor" (Romans 12:10 NRSV).

An example of this kind of love is found between David and Jonathan in the Old Testament:

> When David had finished speaking to Saul, the soul of Jonathan was bound to the soul of David, and Jonathan loved him as his own soul. Saul took him that day and would not let him return to his father's house. Then Jonathan made a covenant with David, because he loved him as his own soul. — *1 Samuel 18:1–3 (NRSV)*

In the Old Testament Hebrew, the corresponding word is *aheb,* which means to have human love toward another person, as a friend.[9] It is also the kind of love God has toward man. Solomon wrote of this kind of *aheb* love, saying, "A friend loves at all times, and a brother is born for a time of adversity" (Proverbs 17:17 NIV).

The word for 'brother' in Proverbs 17:17 above is actually derived from the Hebrew word *ach,* pointing to a direct relative—like a sibling from the same family. But it can also indicate a person from the same tribe or clan. Likewise, *phileo* indicates a deep, friendship type of love as found in a family.

Agape

And finally, there is a very special type of love, mentioned more than two hundred times in the New Testament. This type of love is reserved for the divine: *agape* love. In the Greek, this expression for love is not used for anything other than the love of God and His love toward His created beings.[10]

In John 15:12 Jesus tells His disciples, "This is my commandment: Love each other in the same way I have loved you" (NLT). In this verse, Jesus uses the verb *agapao,*[11] which describes a love that is self-sacrificing—that is, *agape* love, the highest form of love. It is the definition of God's unconditional and immeasurable love for His created beings, and the kind of love Jesus exhibited to mankind by taking man's sin upon Himself and dying on the cross. John affirms this in 1 John 3:16, saying,

We know what real love is because Jesus gave up his life for us. So we also ought to give up our lives for our brothers and sisters. — 1 John 3:16 (NLT)

This kind of love focuses on the will rather than emotions, experience, or libido—because it involves commitment to another person (or other people). In his book *The Almighty: Power, Wisdom, Holiness, Love*, author Donald Bloesch cites Anders Nygren who writes of *agape* love:

> Agape is unmotivated in the sense that it is not contingent on any value or worth in the object of love. It is spontaneous and heedless, for it does not determine beforehand whether love will be effective or appropriate in any particular case.[12]

Agape love is the kind of love Jesus commanded His disciples to show toward their enemies, and thus commands us to do the same: "But I say, love your enemies! Pray for those who persecute you!" (Matthew 5:4 NLT).

What would our lives—and the world—look like if Christians loved like this: sacrificially, spontaneously, and without condition?

The Truth about Agape

Only two of these words are used by the New Testament writers—*agapao* (to have self-sacrificial love, or *agape*), and *phileo* (to have brotherly love, or *philia*).

Let's dig a little deeper into *agape* love. No other book in the Bible speaks more about *agape* than the book of 1 John.

Two important themes come out of 1 John. First, consider 1 John 4:7:

> *Dear friends, let us continue to love one another, for love comes from God. Anyone who loves is a child of God and knows God. (NLT)*

The first thing John clarifies is that it is inconsistent (and actually false) to claim we *agapao*-love God while not *agapao*-loving other Christians. We cannot love God without loving brothers and sisters who also love Him.

The second thing John reveals is that it contradicts God's Word to assert a person *agapao*-loves God if they don't also *obey* Him. Loving God and obeying His instruction are intricately connected. It is impossible to love God but at the same time disregard the instructions He has left in the Word—the Bible. Consider another verse from 1 John:

> *Loving God means keeping his commandments, and his commandments are not burdensome.* — *1 John 5:3 (NLT)*

Loving God and obeying His commands are two activities that cannot be separated. Paul teaches this concept in Galatians 5:14 when he writes: "For the whole law [God's instruction] can be summed up in this one command: 'Love [*agapao*] your neighbor as yourself'" (NLT).

To better understand *agape* love, a few things must be clarified. First, *agape* originates from God, not man. Second, *agape* is sacrificial. Let's start with the concept that *agape* love originates with God.

Agape Love Originates with God

It is this type of love John is referring to in 1 John 4:7–21. John calls believers to love one another, because "love comes from God..." (1 John 4:7 NLT). He says that God is love, and if believers are not loving each other, they are not in God. John uses some pretty harsh terms: anyone who does not love others does not really love God—because ultimately, that person doesn't truly know God's love. In this passage, John does not use the word *phileo*, but rather *agapao*, indicating God's self-sacrificial, unconditional, committed love.

John is clear that this kind of love is unique and special, and it cannot be mustered up by any man; this kind of love comes only from God. He writes, "Dear friends, let us continue to love one another, for love comes from God. Anyone who loves is a child of God and knows God" (1 John 4:7 NLT). From whom does love come? It comes from God.

I know how to work with wood; I love carpentry. But I only know the skills for carpentry because my father taught me. I create things in a very specific way. I shape things. I cut things. I know little tricks of the trade that my father taught me. So, in other words, I do carpentry like my father; my woodworking is reflective of the way my father works with wood. I don't do it like anyone else other than my father.

Now I couldn't say that I do carpentry like my father if my father had never taught me carpentry. If my father had not been the one who taught me, I could say I do carpentry and my father does carpentry, and we do carpentry together sometimes, but I couldn't say I do carpentry like my father. I do a special type of carpentry.

Similarly, this is what John is saying—only magnified! John is saying God wants us to *agapao*-love others, and this kind of love simply cannot be self-produced. It's a godly love that comes from spending time with God the Father. When a person has experienced God's *agape* love, they know what it looks like.

Agape Love Is Sacrificial

> God bestows His blessings without discrimination. The followers of Jesus are children of God, and they should manifest the family likeness by doing good to all, even those who deserve the opposite. — F. F. Bruce[13]

John also makes it clear that *agape* love is sacrificial. It is a radical giving-of-self type of love. We read in 1 John 4:9 that God showed us how much He loved us by sending His one and only Son into the world so that we could have eternal life through Him.

I love how the New Living Translation presents 1 John 4:10: "Not that we loved God, but that he loved us and sent his Son as a sacrifice to take away our sins" (NLT).

This is what real love is. It is a love that says, "I am willing to give up things that I believe I am entitled to and have rights to, because I don't want to cause anyone else to stumble or fall."

This is what Jesus did for us. According to Philippians 2:5–8, Jesus, who was in the "form of God" (Philippians 2:6 NRSV), did not consider equality with God something to hold on to at all costs. Rather, He gave up everything and "emptied himself, taking the form of a slave, being born in human likeness. And being found in human form, he humbled himself and became obedient to the point of death—even death on a cross."

David Nelmes summarizes *agape* love beautifully. He writes:

> Unconditional love that is always giving and impossible to take or be a taker. It devotes total commitment to seek [the other person's] highest best no matter how anyone may respond. This form of love is totally selfless and does not change whether the love given is returned or not.[14]

This is the powerful love God extended to us, and it is this same kind of love He expects us to extend to others. Jesus said, "A new command I give you: Love [*agapao*] one another. As I have loved [*agapao*] you, so you must love one another. By this everyone will know that you are my disciples, if you love one another" (John 13:34–35 NIV).

Why is it so important to love others with *agape* love? *Agape* love expressed to the world is a testimony or a witness of who Jesus' true disciples are.

WORKBOOK

Chapter 1 Questions

Question: Which of your relationships are characterized by *eros*, *storgē*, or *phileo* love?

_____

_____

_____

_____

_____

_____

_____

_____

_____

_____

_____

Question: In what specific ways have you experienced God's *agape* love through another person in your life? When have you *agapao*-loved others?

_____

_____

_____

_____

_____

_____

_____

_____

_____

_____

_____

_____

Action: Never forget that God's love is different from other kinds of love. Let romantic, familial, and brotherly love have their place in your relationships, but praise God for His *agape* love!

Chapter 1 Notes

CHAPTER TWO

Sacrificial Love

A young man named Steve struggled at school. He had been kicked out of class several times for loud behavior—sometimes screaming! A seminary professor who was just down the hall and had heard about Steve's situation decided to help him out a little bit. "I'm going to invite him into my class for the next few days," he thought. And so he met with Steve. He knew Steve was a strong guy, so he asked him, "Steve, you are pretty strong, right?" Steve responded, "Yep. In fact, I do 100 push-ups every single night."

Impressed by that, the professor thought, "Okay, fair enough." He asked Steve if he would be able to do push-ups for the class the next Friday, to which Steve responded, "Sure!" Absolutely."

Friday came and Steve went to class early. He sat in front. When class started, the teacher pulled out a big box of doughnuts. Now these were the good kind of donuts, the Krispy Kreme specials. And it was Friday—the class was excited and looking forward to the weekend.

So the teacher went to the first girl in the first row and asked her, "Cynthia do you want a doughnut?" Cynthia said, "Yes, yes I would love a doughnut!" The teacher turned to Steve, who was at the front of the class, and asked Steve, "Would you do ten push-ups so that Cynthia may have a doughnut?" Cynthia didn't think anything of it and watched Steve as he completed push-ups for her so she could enjoy her donut.

The teacher asked the next person, Joe, if he would like a doughnut. Joe said yes, and again asked if Steve would do ten more push-ups so that Joe could have a doughnut, too. And so it went. The teacher went down the first aisle and the second aisle, before coming to Scott, the captain of the football team and the center of the basketball team. When the teacher asked Scott if he would like a doughnut, Scott's reply was, "Well, I can do the push-ups myself." The teacher responded, "No, Scott, you have to let Steve do the push-ups for you. He's the only one who can do the push-ups for you." Scott replied, "Well I don't want one then!" The teacher told him to leave the donut on his desk and asked if Steve would to go ahead and do ten push-ups for the donut that Scott did not want.

By this time, Steve had begun to slow down a little. He stayed on the floor in between sets because it took too much effort to get up and down. Beads of perspiration glistened on his brow as the teacher started down the third row. Now the students were beginning to grow a bit upset with the teacher, who proceeded to ask Jenny if she wanted a donut. Jenny crossed her arms and said, "No, I don't want a donut." The teacher then asked Steve, "Would you do ten push-ups so Jenny can have a donut that she doesn't want?" Steve managed to do another ten, and Jenny received the donut.

By now every student asked was saying no and many uneaten donuts beckoned students from their desks. Steve was putting forth a lot of effort to get these push-ups done before each next donut was offered. Sweat dripped on the floor beneath his red face. His arms shook with the exertion. Other students wandered in to the classroom to watch the show, and sat along the heaters on the side of the room. When the teacher realized this, he did a quick head check and realized there were thirty-four students in the class. He wondered if Steve would make it.

The teacher went on to the next person, then the next person and the next person—and Steve was progressively having a more difficult time. Finally, the teacher went to the last girl, Susan. With tears flowing down her face, Susan asked, "Can I get down there and help him do those push-ups?" The teacher, with tears now streaming down his own face, said, "No, he has to do them himself. Would you do ten push-ups for Susan, Steve?" Steve did it. As he very slowly finished his last set of push-ups with the understanding that he had accomplished all that was required of him, having done 350 push-ups, his arms buckled beneath him and he fell to the floor.

The teacher turned to his class and said, "So it was when our Savior Jesus Christ prayed to His Father, 'Into thine hands I commend my spirit' with the understanding that He had done everything that was required of Him. Jesus collapsed on the cross and died even for those who didn't want His gift—just like some of you chose not to accept the gift that was provided for you today."[15]

Agape love is sacrificial, and it costs everything.

A Fragrant Offering

The cross is the culmination of what *agape* love looks like, the ultimate act of sacrificial love. Jesus died for every person in the world, regardless of whether they believed Him or not. God stretched out His arms on the cross. This is why Jesus, who exhibited the ultimate sacrificial love, came to earth. Jesus gave His life so that others might live. This is the greatest act of love.

Jesus speaks of the ultimate act of love and what it looks like, saying, "Greater love has no one than this: to lay down one's life for one's friends" (John 15:13 NIV).

The apostle Paul wrote about this in his letters to the various churches. In his letter to the Ephesians, he exhorted Christians to love others in this same, sacrificial way: "and walk in the way of love, just as Christ loved us and gave himself up for us as a fragrant offering and sacrifice to God" (Ephesians 5:2 NIV).

There is something beautiful about sacrificial love—a mystery for us to try to figure out. Paul says it is like a "fragrant offering" to God. Some translations use the term "aroma." In Genesis 8 we read:

> *Then Noah built an altar to the Lord, and took of every clean animal and of every clean bird, and offered burnt offerings on the altar. And when the LORD smelled the pleasing odor, the LORD said in his heart, "I will never again curse the ground because of humankind, for the*

inclination of the human heart is evil from youth; nor will I ever again destroy every living creature as I have done.
— *Genesis 8:20-21 (NRSV)*

The idea that sacrifice is a sweet aroma to God is an ancient concept. When a sacrifice was burnt on an altar, the odor was thought of as going up to the heavens, pleasing the pagan gods. When Noah presented offerings to the Lord, God found the aroma pleasing—so much so that He covenanted never to curse the ground or destroy every living creature again, as He had in the Flood.

Paul uses this Old Testament imagery to teach about Jesus' sacrifice, which was pleasing to God. The word for 'fragrant' is *euodia*, which literally means "a good smell," or a "sweet savor."[16] Metaphorically, it refers to persons or things that are well-pleasing to God.

In another of Paul's letters, one written to the Corinthian church, Paul says, "For we are the aroma of Christ to God among those who are being saved and among those who are perishing" (2 Corinthians 2:15 ESV). For believers, their sacrifice is obedience to God, as they "walk in the way of love [*agapao*]" (Ephesians 5:2 NIV) just as Jesus did. The act of obeying God, listening to His instruction given in the Word of God, and responding accordingly, just as Jesus did by going to the cross, is an act of sacrificial love that is a sweet-smelling aroma to God!

Paul, writing to the Philippian church about how God views obedience, said, "I have all I need and more, now that I have received your gifts from Epaphroditus. They are a sweet smelling aroma, an acceptable sacrifice, well-pleasing to God" (Philippians 4:18 BSB).

The Aroma of Life

Wherever there is true love, there must be giving, and giving to the point of sacrifice. Love is not satisfied with giving trinkets; it must give at the cost of sacrifice: it must give blood, life, all. And it was so with the love of God: "He so loved the world, that He gave his only-begotten Son." Christ also loved and gave Himself up, an offering and a sacrifice to God. — F. B. Meyer[17]

In ancient Roman times, there was something known as a "triumph." A triumph was a procession performed after Rome had experienced victory in war, where various participants marched through Roman streets in a specific order: state officials and the senate, the trumpeters, those who carried the spoils of war, pictures and models of the conquered land, and then animals for sacrifice. Princes and leaders who were taken captive in the war followed in chains, and then the "lectors" who carried decorated rods with axes that symbolized the power to carry out capital punishment over the captives. Priests carrying censors they swung back and forth, filled with incense, produced a sweet-smelling aroma that everyone watching would smell. Lastly, the general himself, dressed in purple (signifying royalty and victory), carried in an ornate chariot, made his way down the streets. All the people would declare in unity, "Triumph! Triumph!"[18]

This victory procession is the imagery Paul is drawing from when he calls Christ's death a "sweet smelling aroma, an acceptable sacrifice" (Philippians 4:18 BSB). The imagery of the perfume Roman citizens smelled as the priests made way for the victorious general signified life and victory in Christ. For those who believe in Jesus, the smell of sacrifice is a sweet aroma of life; for those who don't, it is the odor of death.

This sacrificial love is what believers are to imitate. Second Peter 1:4 says, "For by these He has granted to us His precious and magnificent promises, so that by them you may become partakers of the divine nature, having escaped the corruption that is in the world by lust" (NASB). When a person receives Jesus into their life, His very life becomes their nature, unifying with their spirit (see Colossians 3). Christ's nature within us makes it possible for us to love sacrificially, as Jesus loves.

Jesus gave His all so that those who believe Him may live. Jesus made a way by paying a steep price so that you and I would have an opportunity to choose eternal life over death. This is what *agape* love looks like. It's a love that brings a fullness of life both in the eternal and in the here and now. This is the love of God—a love that is always seeking to bring life to others.

Chapter 2 Questions

Question: How do you sacrifice in your love to God? What more might He be asking you to sacrifice for Him?

_____

_____

_____

_____

_____

_____

_____

_____

_____

_____

_____

_____

Question: How do you sacrifice in your love for others? To whom could you show deeper *agape* love, and how?

_____

_____

_____

_____

_____

_____

_____

_____

_____

_____

_____

_____

_____

Action: Love God and others till it hurts! Let your *agape* love toward Him and others be a sweet-smelling, daily offering to the Lord.

Chapter 2 Notes

CHAPTER THREE

What Love Looks Like

I am not sure exactly what heaven will be like, but I know that when we die and it comes time for God to judge us, he will not ask, "How many good things have you done in your life?" Rather he will ask, "How much love did you put into what you did?" — **Mother Teresa**[19]

Consider Paul, who had come to the end of his first missionary journey with Barnabas. The Jerusalem council had met to decide what should be required of Gentile converts (Acts 15:1–29), and Paul and Barnabas had experienced a difference of opinion and had decided it was time to go their separate ways. This began Paul's second missionary journey, and much of the focus of this journey involved visiting some of the fledgling churches that had started as a result of his first journey.

One of those churches was in Corinth, the capital city of the Roman province of Achaia. This province included much of modern-day Greece. In Paul's day, Corinth had become a crossroads of trade, both by land and by sea, and was thus a bustling commercial center. Luxuries from all over the world could be found in Corinth—and likewise, worldly corruptions. The temple of Aphrodite (the Greek goddess of love) stood nearby, an emblem of the immorality that had taken over the city.

Paul had already left Corinth, only to find out while in Ephesus that the Corinthian church was experiencing division. The people were fighting over whose spiritual giftings were better, and pride was rampant. On top of that, the Corinthian church had begun to exhibit immoral behavior, like the secular world around them.

Paul did not beat around the bush in addressing this issue with the church in Corinth. Paul was very clear that the way the church had been "loving" people was not godly love. The way that they had been backbiting and arguing about whose gift was better, the deep dissension and disunity in the church, and the proliferation of arrogance and pride infecting believers who were living sexually immoral lives—that wasn't real, godly, *agapao* love! And so he clarified what real love looks like.

Thirteen chapters into this letter to the Corinthians, Paul wrote what has become popularly known in Christian circles as the "love chapter." Though it has become a nice set of verses to put on wedding invitations, Paul's intent behind the verses was to reveal what true love is: true love reflects the character of God.

Love is patient; love is kind; love is not envious or boastful or arrogant or rude. It does not insist on its own way; it is not irritable or resentful; it does not rejoice in wrongdoing, but rejoices in the truth. It bears all things, believes all things, hopes all things, endures all things.

— *1 Corinthians 13:4–7 (NRSV)*

Paul thus painted a beautiful tapestry of what God's love is and what God's love is not. In fact, there are fifteen verbs used in this short four-verse passage of Scripture. God's love is *active*. Do not miss this point of God's love: He acts for the benefit of *others*, regardless of how they respond to Him.

Love Is Patient and Kind

What does Christ-like love look like, when applied to our lives? Paul begins his list of what God's love is by saying godly love is patient and kind. The word 'patient' in the original Greek, *makrothymeo*, means "to be of a long spirit; not to lose heart. To persevere patiently and bravely enduring misfortunes and troubles. To be patient in bearing the offenses and injuries of others, and be slow in avenging."[20]

Consider what happened at the cross—what a place of injustice! Jesus did not deserve to be there. His own Jewish people spit in His face and yet He showed love. They forced a crown of thorns upon His head and flogged Him—almost to death—and yet He showed love, persevering and avenging not. This is the same kind of patient love Paul says we are to exhibit toward others, especially those who offend and persecute us.

In Galatians 5:22–23, Paul lists kindness as one of the fruits of the Spirit. In this scripture, the word 'kindness' in the original Greek is the word *chrestotes*, which means to act benevolently toward others.[21] Kindness of this sort is more than a nice note to a friend. God's kindness is exhibited in His act of saving those He loves—not because of what they have done—but because of mercy (see Titus 3:4–5). This act of love is the greatest example of kindness the world will ever know!

Love Is Not Envious or Boastful

While it's good to know what God's love *is*, it's also instructive to consider what His love is *not*. First, God's love is not envious or boastful. Some versions say love "is not jealous." To be jealous comes from the word *zeloo*, which means to "be heated or to boil with envy, hatred or anger."[22] Godly love is not rooted in rivalry against another person, but rejoices in their successes! To be boastful simply means to brag about one's self, or to extol one's self excessively.

If the church is to express God's love, jealousy and pride have no place in the life of the believer. Each of these character traits places the self above others, as if to say, "I don't care about you; I am going to make myself more important than you." These behaviors show that the individual would rather elevate themselves and their agenda above that of anyone else. But this was not the attitude of Jesus Christ (see Philippians 2).

Love Is Not Arrogant

Moreover, God's love is not arrogant. C.S. Lewis once wrote, "A proud man is always looking down on things and people; and of course, as long as you're looking down, you can't see something that's above you."[23] Paul knew this and was firm in redirecting the Corinthian church toward casting aside their pride and humbling themselves before God.

Everyone has likely become nauseated from being around people who are arrogant—who are so puffed up on themselves that they can't see much past their own nose. According to Merriam-Webster's Dictionary, the word 'arrogant' means "having or showing the insulting attitude of people who believe they are better, smarter or more important than other people."[24] Have you ever felt above someone else? Better than others? According to the Holy Scriptures, this is not Christ-like love.

King Solomon, the wisest man of all time, penned these words: "Pride goes before destruction, a haughty spirit before a fall" (Proverbs 16:18 NIV) and "Haughty eyes and a proud heart, the lamp of the wicked, are sin!" (Proverbs 21:4 ESV). An inflated, puffed-up attitude is sin, according to God, and He will discipline those who are caught in this circle of self-focused behavior. In fact, the psalmist writes that God will "rebuke the arrogant, who are accursed, those who stray from your commands" (Psalms 119:21 NIV).

Jesus demonstrated the opposite of arrogance, humbly laying down His life as a servant to humankind. Philippians 2:8 says He "humbled himself by becoming obedient to death—even death on a cross!" (NIV). Do we humble ourselves like Christ, or do we set our wants and needs above others?

Love Is Not Rude

Yet another non-characteristic of love is rudeness: love is not rude. To be rude comes from an interesting Greek word, *aschemoneo*, which means "to act unbecomingly."[25] Unbecoming behavior that does not draw people to God, but rather reflects an "unbecoming" image that is not Christ, is not self-sacrificing, selfless love!

Instead, believers' behavior should draw people to Jesus. Their behavior, attitude, and character should be "a Christ-like fragrance rising up to God" (2 Corinthians 2:15 NLT) that Paul says is "perceived differently by those who are being saved and by those who are perishing. … But to those who are being saved, we are a life-giving perfume" (2 Corinthians 2:15–16a NLT).

For example, coming alongside others who are hurting with a kind word or an embrace reflects Christ to others. A grace-filled, loving attitude that is not rude to others reflects Christ. A person attracts others by the qualities he or she displays; a person keeps others close by the qualities he or she possesses.[26] Displaying unbecoming behavior does not draw people to Christ, but possessing *agape* love does!

Love Does Not Insist on Its Own Way

T.S. Eliot wisely said, "Half the harm that is done in this world is caused by people who want to feel important."[27] This is so true, and it was no different in Paul's day. Paul warned the Corinthians about the trouble with insisting on getting one's own way, of this desire to "be important." In Paul's letter to the Philippians he writes, "Don't be selfish; don't try to impress others. Be humble, thinking of others as better than yourselves. Don't look out only for your own interests, but take an interest in others, too" (Philippians 2:3–4 NLT). And then he tells the Philippians what attitude they should have: "You must have the same attitude that Christ Jesus had" (Philippians 2:5 NLT).

Jesus did not elevate His rights or His privileges or His stature over anyone! How often do we feel like we have a certain right that we will fight for? The right to be heard? The right to fairness? The right to life? Jesus could have felt that way, too, and as God in the flesh, He could have demanded justice. Of all people, He did not deserve to go to the cross; He was without sin. Yet He who knew no sin became sin for you and for me, enduring suffering and shame and ridicule on the cross.

In 1 Corinthians 13, Paul is clear that love does not demand its own way. Love doesn't say, "I have an agenda here, and I'm going to demand it is met." *Agapao* love brings with it the idea of giving up one's rights and one's privileges for the sake of others; in essence, this is what Paul calls the church to do earlier in 1 Corinthians 10.

In 1 Corinthians 10:24 Paul told the Corinthians not to be concerned for their own good but for the good of others. How often do Christians walk around thinking their attitude is their own prerogative? We might be tempted to think, "If it's not obviously harming someone else, why care?" At times, people do what's best for themselves, rather than doing what's best for others and their salvation.

Not insisting on one's own way requires an attitude that looks out. It looks to see who is lost, hurting, and needing Christ. It is not prideful and doesn't demand its own way. It's an attitude that turns to Scripture and asks: How am I going to serve God, in a way that benefits others?

Love Doesn't Hold Grudges

Because God's kind of love doesn't insist on its own way, loving as God loves also requires us to guard ourselves against possessing an irritable, begrudging demeanor. In other words, we must not be one who is easily angered or who holds grudges. If we harbor something in offense when we have been wronged or hurt and we choose not to forgive, we are not loving as God loves. Jesus forgave even His enemies who were crucifying Him "for they don't know what they are doing" (Luke 23:34 NLT).

Instead, godly love recognizes the need for others to be forgiven and subsequently pours out grace to others—even those who are hard to love!

Jesus modeled what it means to forgive when He taught His disciples the Lord's Prayer. He said we are not to pray empty, meaningless prayers with many meaningless words—for God already knows what we need before we ask! Rather, He called us to pray for His kingdom to be established on earth as it already is in heaven, for provision and for forgiveness—"as we also have forgiven our debtors" (Matthew 6:12 NRSV). When "we confess our sins, He is faithful and righteous to forgive us" (1 John 1:9 NASB).

When we forgive others when they sin against us, Matthew 6:14–15 says, "your heavenly Father will also forgive you. But if you do not forgive others their sins, your Father will not forgive your sins" (NIV).

If you don't think that's truth, look to what Jesus says in the parable about the master who forgave the debt owed him by another person (Matthew 18:21–35). That slave went to the other slave who owed him a smaller debt and demanded, "Give me the money." The master found out about it and said, "Didn't I forgive you of a huge debt? Yet you have the audacity to go to one of your fellow servants to demand a small debt? How dare you!"

But the parable doesn't end there. The master gave the slave the punishment he deserved because of his unwillingness to forgive his fellow servants. Jesus says this is how the Kingdom of God will be!

God is a forgiving God, but He makes it very clear— we set the standard by which He forgives in our own life. This begs the question from each of us: *Are we* truly forgiving others?

Love Doesn't Rejoice in Wrongdoing

Because the Word is the means that God uses to speak to us, we need to love it and use it. — **Daniel Hyde**[28]

Rejoicing in immorality is the final element in the list of what God says love "does not do." Some translations say, "Love does not delight in evil but rejoices with the truth" (1 Corinthians 13:6 NIV). Keep in mind that Paul was writing to the Corinthian church, which was surrounded by a culture neck-deep in immorality, sin, and evil practices. Paul knew these new Christians were struggling with being seduced into their old ways—how true this is for us, too!

Paul reminds these Christians that real love does not find contentment in evil, but in truth. God is "not a God who delights in wickedness" (Psalm 5:4 ESV), but who desires truth "in the inward being" (Psalm 51:6 ESV).

Perhaps this is why Paul taught how important it is to focus on what is good, holy, and righteous throughout many of his letters.

And now, dear brothers and sisters, one final thing. Fix your thoughts on what is true, and honorable, and right, and pure, and lovely, and admirable. Think about things that are excellent and worthy of praise. — *Philippians 4:8 (NLT)*

The psalmist, too, gave instruction on what the believer's attitude should be concerning truth versus evil:

Happy are those who do not follow the advice of the wicked, or take the path that sinners tread, or sit in the seat of scoffers; but their delight is in the law of the LORD, and on his law they meditate day and night. — Psalm 1:1–2 (NRSV)

Godly love focuses on the truth of God's Word—the law of the Lord. Are you struggling with a world that seems corrupt and hopeless? Turn to God's Word to find the plumb line of what is right and good. Those who rejoice in the truth (1 Corinthians 13:6) focus on God's Word moment by moment as they walk through life; it is what brings them joy and thus what enables them to love as God loves. Are you rejoicing in God's truth?

Love Believes, Hopes, and Endures

Love is not irritable, and it doesn't hold grudges. Love forgives. Love is patient, and it is not jealous or prideful. Nor does love rejoice in evil, but instead it celebrates the things of God—for God is holy, and He cannot be in the presence of man's filth, sin, and disobedience.

Yet because God's nature is *agape*—selfless, sacrificial, and committed love—He made a way to be in relationship with us, interceding for us while we were yet sinners. He bore our sins and endured their consequences on the cross.

The question is, how can we do the same for others? If we want to love others as Christ does, we must be willing and able to bear and endure anything. And we must maintain our hope and belief—for anything is possible with God (Matthew 19:26)!

A Love That Restores

Jesus Christ became Incarnate for one purpose, to make
a way back to God that man might stand before Him as
he was created to do, the friend and lover of God Himself.
— **Oswald Chambers**[29]

One way we can be like Christ—bearing all things,
hoping all things, and enduring all things—is through the
ministry of reconciliation. It was for the restoration of the
world that the ultimate sacrifice, Jesus Christ, came and
died on the cross. This was the ultimate act of selfless,
reconciliatory *agape* love that God the Father exhibited
toward His created beings.

The prophet Isaiah said:

*Rather, your iniquities have been barriers between you
and your God, and your sins have hidden his face from
you so that he does not hear.* — *Isaiah 59:2 (NRSV)*

Every person who has not received forgiveness of sin
through belief in Christ remains in this destitute
condition—a place of being separate from God. Sin
creates a "barrier" between God and the person. God
cannot stomach sin and filth. And so not only did God
come to forgive, but God came in the form of Jesus to
restore and transform. Then, after Jesus was crucified,
entombed, and resurrected, He left a deposit—His Holy
Spirit, who indwells those who trust in Him. This Holy
Spirit enables the believer to be reconciled, changed, and

in right relationship with God. To share the forgiveness of God without sharing the grace of transformation is to share only part of the Gospel of Jesus Christ—we have victory because sin and its grip upon us has been defeated (see Romans 8)!

God in His great mercy and love provided people a way out of sin and eternal separation from Him. This is *agape* love in action! And the most powerful way people can love others as God loves them is to point others toward the way out. We are never more like Christ than when we love another person by helping to reconcile them with their Creator by accepting Jesus as the Savior who offers forgiveness of sin and restoration of our souls:

> You demonstrate biblical love when you take steps to restore a fellow-believer overtaken in sin. This not only encourages a fallen believer to return to his first love of Jesus Christ, but it also gives others involved in the restoration process on-going opportunities to examine the depth of their love to the Lord. — **John C. Broger**[30]

Agape love is not defined by man; it's more than a nice hug or a handshake. Those can be part of brotherly *philia* love, and could even be a *storgē* type of familial love— like the love of a parent or grandparent, brother or sister. These types of love are beautiful and great, but God did not say to come and share *storgē* love. He did not come to this earth and depart with a command to share *philia* love or *eros* love. No, God said He came to exhibit *agape* love. And He calls His followers to do the same.

This *agape* love is what will bring about the restoration of the church, and ultimately the restoration of the world. If we are to see the Kingdom of God come and His will be done on this earth, it will come from His church sharing His true *agape* love with others—and without apology.

WORKBOOK

Chapter 3 Questions

Question: In which specific aspects of your relationships or life are you most prone to act unlovingly? Which items from the 1 Corinthians 13 "love is not..." list prove most challenging to you?

_____

_____

_____

_____

_____

_____

_____

_____

_____

_____

_____

Question: To what lengths would you go to share God's restoring love with someone? What's one difficult thing

you might need to endure in your life right now in order
to love another (or others) God's way?

_____

_____

_____

_____

_____

_____

_____

_____

_____

_____

Action: Go out of your way to be patient and kind to
others. Then figure out what makes you react in envious,
boastful, arrogant, rude, irritable, or resentful ways, and
lean on God's love to overcome those challenges.
Likewise, pray and find strength in the Word and the
Spirit to resist the world's many temptations to enjoy
things God says are wrong. In place of sin, embrace God's
truth and let His love restore your heart, your life, and—
ultimately—the church.

Chapter 3 Notes

CHAPTER FOUR

Tough Love

Love precedes discipline. — John Owen[31]

From 1 Corinthians chapter 13, we've discovered that God's kind of love isn't always easy to give, nor is it always easy to receive. Have you ever heard the fascinating story of how giraffes enter this world?

Giraffes are very tall animals, the torso of their body being far off the ground when they stand. The mother giraffe, surprisingly, does not lay down to give birth to a baby giraffe.

The mother giraffe tries her best to prepare a soft area—bushes or soft dirt—and gives birth standing up. The baby giraffe starts its journey down the birth canal and then literally falls, approximately six feet or so, from the mother to the ground, its little legs clustered up underneath it.

After the calf is born, the mother giraffe goes over to the baby to make sure no predators are a threat there and then proceeds to do the most unimaginable thing with her very strong legs: she gently kicks her baby across the ground to help it get up and be able to stand and walk.

And that little baby giraffe begins to topple over and move across this hard dirt, this hard ground. The newborn giraffe doesn't stand up immediately after the fall, so the mother giraffe lovingly goes over to the baby giraffe and kicks it again to the point where the baby giraffe then has to stand up on its own little legs.

In the wild, if that baby giraffe doesn't learn immediately how to stand, it won't learn how to run; if it doesn't know how to run, then it will potentially meet an early death.[32]

Sometimes what we perceive as being hateful, mean, or cruel is actually for our own good, as in the case of the mother giraffe and her baby. And sometimes a harsh-seeming act can, in fact, be a generous act of genuine love—*tough* love. To be honest, it's kind of hard for us to think that love can or should be tough at times. Perhaps this is because in our humanness, we naturally fall back on love being a feeling, which we assume should always be good.

However, as C.S. Lewis wrote, "Though our feelings come and go, God's love for us does not."[33] It's hard to make sense of the fact that love could even come in the form of chastisement or discipline!

Sometimes *agape* love appears to be tough love.

The Rod That Strikes

There are moments in our lives that we need people to express love in such hard-seeming ways for the sake of our health and our well-being. When we look to God's Word to understand what divine love looks like, we clearly find that the type of love Jesus shows is sometimes just plain tough.

Jesus started on his way, a man ran up to him and fell on his knees before him. "Good teacher," he asked, "what must I do to inherit eternal life? "Why do you call me good?" Jesus answered. "No one is good—except God alone. You know the commandments: 'You shall not murder, you shall not commit adultery, you shall not steal, you shall not give false testimony, you shall not defraud, honor your father and mother.'" "Teacher," he declared, "all these I have kept since I was a boy." Jesus looked at him and loved him. "One thing you lack," he said. "Go, sell everything you have and give to the poor, and you will have treasure in heaven. Then come, follow me." At this the man's face fell. He went away sad, because he had great wealth. Jesus looked around and said to his disciples, "How hard it is for the rich to enter the kingdom of God!" The disciples were amazed at his words. But Jesus said again, "Children, how hard it is to enter the kingdom of God! It is easier for a camel to go through the eye of a needle than for someone who is rich to enter the kingdom of God." The disciples were even more amazed, and said to each other, "Who then can be saved?" — Mark 10:17–26 (NIV)

Jesus was interacting with a rich young ruler, who genuinely wanted to know what he needed to do to inherit eternal life. Jesus' response, however, took the man aback. "Go, sell everything you have and give to the poor, and you will have treasure in heaven. Then come, follow me." Scripture says the man's face "fell." Mark used the Greek word *stygnazō* here, meaning "to be sad" or "to be sorrowful."[34] The rich young ruler wanted eternal life, but not enough to give up all of his material possessions here on earth. Jesus' response, however, was filled with genuine love: Scripture says he looked at the man "and loved him."

The word for this type of love, in the original Greek, is *egapesen*.[35] This word is related to the same verb, *agapao*, as the word for godly love—*agape*. In this passage of Scripture, what we find is this peculiar Greek word that basically means to act out the love of God in a way that considers what's taking place. In other words, Jesus loved this man by gathering information from the situation at hand and expressing godly love out of it. This is *egapesen*.

This shapes the way we look at the whole story!

Now who is this rich ruler? Well, the Gospels don't reveal much, but what we do know is the reaction that this rich ruler had. At first, he runs to see Jesus, kneels before Him, and is excited to follow Him. And to be honest, the social strata were similar to how they are today: you would be hard-pressed to see a rich person be undignified and grow excited about anything!

But here a rich ruler runs to kneel before a controversial rabbi. "What must I do to inherit the kingdom of God?" he asks.

Jesus proceeds to meet this young man where he is, asking questions to which He already knows the answers.

You know the commandments, right? The law of Moses? You've kept those, right? And Jesus begins listing them off. Yes, of course! This man knows his Hebrew Scriptures. But he is lacking one thing: love that will sacrifice anything, even worldly wealth, for God and to show His love to others.

Jesus looks at this man, whose heart is longing to do good but who is coming up short, and shows him real love in His response. Genuine love doesn't hear a situation and go, "Wow! You are doing great things and you look good to great people! You receive accolades from everyone around you! That's good enough!" No, Jesus knows what it takes to enter the Kingdom of God. He's the gatekeeper, if you will. Remember, Jesus Himself said, "No one can come to the Father except through me" (John 14:6 NLT). To enter the Kingdom of God, one must follow Jesus wholeheartedly—relinquishing everything of this world.

Genuine *agape* love is brave enough to point out where someone comes up short, especially regarding their eternal destiny. That kind of loving "discipline" may be hard, but listen to what Solomon says about the importance of disciplining a child: "Do not withhold discipline from a child; if you strike him with a rod, he will not die" (Proverbs 23:13 ESV). There is blessing that comes from discipline.

Sometimes the Lord's discipline, or even His commands, will feel like harsh reproof—like being struck with a rod. However, the Lord disciplines those He loves:

And have you forgotten the exhortation that addresses you as sons? "My son, do not regard lightly the discipline

of the Lord, nor be weary when reproved by him. For the
Lord disciplines the one he loves, and chastises every son
whom he receives." — Hebrews 12:5-6 (ESV)

We cannot separate God's love from His discipline; discipline is evidence of love. Sometimes that discipline will come in the form of speaking truth to those who are not following God, or who are believers but choose to distance themselves from Him. Consider what John MacArthur says: "Discipline is difficult, painful, and often heartrending. It is not that we should not love the offenders, but that we should love Christ, His church, and His Word even more. Our love to the offenders is not to be sentimental tolerance, but correcting love (cf. Prov 27:6)."[36] This is how Jesus loves us, and this is how we should, in turn, love others.

We often learn more of God under the rod that strikes us than under the staff that comforts us. — **Stephen Charnock**[37]

Genuine Love

I went to Olivet Nazarene University right out of high school. To be honest, I approached college life just like I think a lot of young men probably would—like summer camp. I was excited to go! I wanted to be social and involved and around people, and like any young man, I was excited to see all the young women at college—so much so that I would date a different girl every single week. I wish this were not true, but it is. By my sophomore year, I was a pro. I journeyed over to the freshman girls' dorm to see all the new girls coming in. I wasn't the only one.

Somehow, they already knew about me. They would say, "Don't talk to AJ, he's a player," or "Don't talk to AJ, he's a womanizer." I was offended! And I was angry. Why were people labeling me a player? Why were they calling me a womanizer? That's not nice! I mean, just because I didn't want to get married to these women, I was a player? Most of my friends sided with me, affirming to me that I wasn't a bad guy and I wasn't doing anything wrong. But I had one friend who loved me enough and cared for me enough to tell me the truth. His name was Adam.

I remember complaining to Adam and expecting him to go, "Oh man, that's messed up! Who do they think they are?" But instead, Adam's response rocked my world: "Well, what did you expect? You *are* a womanizer! You *are* a player!" I opened my mouth, but my thoughts were so jumbled that nothing came out. "You date another girl every other week—come on!" he said. "Why would you think otherwise? You treat women like objects." His words stung, and my ego was smashed. And I was embarrassed—in front of Adam, but more importantly, before God.

I was a man of God! I was going to Olivet Nazarene University, for crying out loud! I didn't want to be known for treating women like objects. Initially I thought, "This isn't going to break our friendship, but I don't know how close we are going to be from this point on." But over time I came to realize what a good friend Adam was for speaking into my life. Adam loved me enough to speak the hard truth of what I was doing. His actions not only didn't break our friendship, they made it stronger; in fact, he ended up being one of the groomsmen at my wedding. What Adam did for me—his act of showing me genuine, godly love—is now a part of my testimony of faith. It was part of the journey of how God transformed me, and lead to me finally humbling myself before God, on my knees, and begging, "God, would You change this heart?"

What Does Tough Love Look Like?

Tough love is exactly what Adam demonstrated toward me: it's tough for the one receiving it, and often it is tough for the person extending it. Parents experience this when rearing children: sometimes a parent must take something away from a child, or set restrictions for a child out of deep love. The child might not be happy about the situation, but the parent is able to look past the immediate and see how certain discipline will benefit the child in the future.

As Christians, we sometimes shy away from tough love toward other believers. It can be challenging to face rejection from someone in your life who doesn't want to hear the truth! Is it worth it to remain comfortable at the expense of a person's walk with the Lord—or worse yet, at the expense of their salvation? Those are tough questions, but questions every believer should contemplate.

Though we never should be flinging condemnation around, we need to trust God when a brother or sister is walking a path that will lead to destruction, and to speak with humility and grace—not with harsh, demeaning or self-elevating judgment (this is the difference between condemnation and caring conviction).

Painful discipline from God may not seem like love. Hebrews 12:11 says, "All discipline for the moment seems not to be joyful, but sorrowful" (NASB). However, don't miss one powerful word in that verse: seems. There is something beneath the dark canopy of sorrow, something good that God is using for His purposes. The writer of Hebrews also says, "My son, do not make light of the Lord's discipline, and do not lose heart when he rebukes you, because the Lord disciplines the one he loves, and he chastens everyone he accepts as his son" (Hebrews 12:5–6 NIV; see also Proverbs 3:11–12).

Suffering and pain, though also byproducts of original sin in the world, may be what God allows to chasten us. It may be His response to a certain sin in our life, or what He uses to humble us that we might be vessels ready to be used by Him for His glory. It may also be something He allows us to experience—like cancer, a death of a loved one, or a financial loss—so that we may be able to comfort others "with the comfort we ourselves receive from God" (2 Corinthians 1:4 NIV).

When experiencing God's tough love, rather than fighting it or complaining, embrace the knowledge that God disciplines those He dearly loves.

A Narrow Gate

For the gate is narrow and the road is hard that leads to life, and there are few who find it. — **Matthew 7:14 (NRSV)**

Where you wind up in eternity will be determined by the road you take here on earth. — **Alan Carr**[38]

When you're experiencing God's tough love, remember too that this life on earth is not much more than a temporary stop—a pause connecting two eternities. No one can escape death, and everyone is surrounded by it. You and I will one day pass from this world. James, the half-brother of Jesus, contemplated this: "Yet you do not know what your life will be like tomorrow. You are just a vapor that appears for a little while and then vanishes away" (James 4:14 NASB).

Jesus makes it very clear that the way to heaven is narrow, while the way to hell is broad. There is a right and a wrong road, and Jesus said the correct road is the narrow one. Look at what Jesus says in Matthew 7:13–14: "Enter through the narrow gate; for the gate is wide and the way is broad that leads to destruction, and there are many who enter through it. For the gate is small and the way is narrow that leads to life, and there are few who find it" (NASB).

In Matthew 7:14, Jesus said that "the gate is narrow" (NRSV). The Greek word here for 'gate' is *pylē*, and refers to a pair of double gates, such as the gates of a town, a palace, a temple, a prison—or even, metaphorically, the "gates" of hell.[39]

Some people scoff at this teaching—because with it comes the truth that Jesus is the only way to heaven. It sounds exclusive and elitist, narrow minded. In 2001, George Barna reported that 51 percent of Americans believed that if a person was generally good, or did enough good things for others during their life, they would move on to eternity with a place secured for them in heaven.[40] Yet this is not what Jesus taught; His way was narrow.

Christians must be "narrow-minded" when it comes to defending the faith regarding the true way, truth and life (John 14:6). That may seem harsh, but the repercussions are worse—eternal separation from God. Sadly, some will choose this path. Jesus said, "Not everyone who says to Me, 'Lord, Lord,' shall enter the kingdom of heaven, but he who does the will of My Father who is in heaven" (Matthew 7:21 NKJV). Why?

Because there is only one gate: *Jesus.*

One of the greatest tools the enemy uses today is deception. Satan convinces people to believe any path they choose, whatever path works for them, is the way to heaven. That's a broad path, right?

But Jesus *agapao*-loves His children so much that He tells us no, the gate is narrow and only a few will enter through it. He loves us enough to tell us the truth instead of what makes us feel good at the time, and we need to do the same for other people. Sometimes, God will kick and prod like that mother giraffe to move people along so they will open their eyes and believe this. This is genuine love.

Genuine love is not only tough sometimes, but it also pulls people from the path of hell. This is the call of the church, and it is our call to one another. Would you care enough to push a person off a train track when a train was coming that would likely kill them? Do you care for others in your family, congregation, workplace, and friend circles enough to push them off the broad path that leads to destruction and toward the narrow path and gate that lead to life?

If my four-year-old daughter or one-year-old son were reaching toward a hot stove and about to place their hand on a red-hot burner, I would run to stop them! I love them more than anything, and love them enough to keep them from going down that road. Genuine love pulls people from the path of hell. Jude directs us, "Rescue others by snatching them from the flames of judgment" (Jude 1:23 NLT).

...for the LORD knows the way of the righteous, but the way of the wicked will perish. — Psalm 1:6 (ESV)

The gate is narrow, and the road is not easy. However, as the Geneva Study Bible says, "Presenting a rosy picture of the Christian life and minimizing that it is filled with trouble does not follow the lead of our Lord."[41] Who could say the life of a Christian is easy, when it's centered on Jesus, who was put to death on a cross? No, the road is hard, but it leads to life.

Whom Will You Serve?

John chapter 6 reflects the mark of genuine love that we learn from Jesus. Jesus has just finished multiplying the loaves and the fish to feed thousands of people—who with full tummies and wondering hearts are ready to hear from this peculiar rabbi. A mega church, in the hills of Galilee!

Jesus gives the people what they want, and moves on to give them what they *need*: true food that satisfies—the Word of God. He begins preaching to them a difficult message that was so unpopular that people started to leave. John attested to this affirming that "Many of his disciples said, 'This is very hard to understand. How can anyone accept it?'" (John 6:60 NLT).

Jesus was well aware His disciples were complaining so He said to them:

> Does this offend you? Then what if you were to see the Son of Man ascending to where he was before? It is the spirit that gives life; the flesh is useless. The words that I have spoken to you are spirit and life. But among you there are some who do not believe." For Jesus knew from the first who were the ones that did not believe, and who was the one that would betray him. And he said, "For this reason I have told you that no one can come to me unless it is granted by the Father." — *John 6:61–65 (NRSV)*

At this point, many disciples did leave Him, no longer following Him. Then, Jesus turned to the twelve and asked them if they were going to leave, too.

Simon Peter replied, "Lord, to whom would we go? You have the words of life that give eternal life. We believe, and we know you are the Holy One of God." — John 6:68–69 NLT)

Good job, Peter!

Jesus could have told those masses of people what they wanted to hear so He could keep the numbers. Sadly, many churches today sacrifice truth for what is comfortable and what will keep people in the church pew. But instead, Jesus loved those listening enough to tell them what they needed—even when it was hard to swallow and unpopular.

Paul the Apostle understood this. Paul's goal was never to win the approval of people, but of God. In Galatians 1:10 Paul writes, "Obviously, I am not trying to win the approval of people, but of God. If pleasing people were my goal, I would not be Christ's servant" (NLT). Those who follow Jesus need to ask themselves the same question: Whom am I serving, and whose approval am I seeking?

This message was not new for Israel, and it is certainly not new for us. After leading Israel into the promised land, Joshua commissioned the nation to make a choice:

*Now therefore revere the LORD, and serve him in sincerity and in faithfulness; put away the gods that your ancestors served beyond the River and in Egypt, and serve the LORD. Now if you are unwilling to serve the LORD, **choose this day whom you will serve**, whether the gods your ancestors served in the region beyond the River or the gods of the Amorites in whose land you are*

living; but as for me and my household, we will serve the
LORD. —Joshua 24:14–15 (NRSV, emphasis added)

Whom do you serve? Is it God? Or yourself?

Do you serve yourself in a way that says, "I don't know if I want to speak into people's lives because that's unpopular and I don't know how people will respond"? Or do you think, "I don't know if love should look tough; I want to make people feel comfortable"? Well then, whom are you serving? Are you trying to please people, or are you pleasing God?

Instead, maybe begin praying, "Lord, reshape my identity and my understanding of what love looks like! Help me not to care about what others think, but only what expresses *agape* love to You and others." Pray for God's help in choosing the faithful way so that you can say with the psalmist:

I have chosen the faithful way; I have placed Your
ordinances before me. — Psalm 119:30 (NASB)

Sometimes the way of God's love *is* tough. But that's because love cares enough to grab a person from the path of hell to put them on the narrow way—on an upward trajectory toward heaven.

WORKBOOK

Chapter 4 Questions

Question: When have you been shown tough love? How did you respond? How did it work to your benefit?

_____

_____

_____

_____

_____

_____

_____

_____

_____

_____

_____

Question: Whom do you need to show tough love for God? What will your first step be?

_____

_____

_____

_____

_____

_____

_____

_____

_____

_____

_____

_____

Action: Accept God's tough love as a sign of His love for you, His child, and resolve to learn the lessons He intends from His discipline. Remembering that life on earth is only a brief stop on the narrow road to eternity, ask God to show you when your family members, friends, or other people in your life need tough love more than anything. At all times, know without a doubt that God is the sole master of your life—now let your actions prove it!

Chapter 4 Notes

CHAPTER FIVE

Transformation

Lemony Snicket wrote in *The Austere Academy* about the dangers of assuming:

> Assumptions are dangerous things to make, and like all dangerous things to make—bombs, for instance, or strawberry shortcake—if you make even the tiniest mistake you can find yourself in terrible trouble. Making assumptions simply means believing things are a certain way with little or no evidence that shows you are correct, and you can see at once how this can lead to terrible trouble. For instance, one morning you might wake up and make the assumption that your bed was in the same place that it always was, even though you would have no real evidence that this was so. But when you got out of your bed, you might discover that it had floated out to sea, and now you would be in terrible trouble all because of the incorrect assumption that you'd made. You can see that it is better not to make too many assumptions, particularly in the morning.[42]

Though Snicket's take on assumptions is a bit extreme and silly, the truth is human beings by nature constantly make assumptions. To assume something is to have little evidence that that thing is true while operating in a way that shows you believe it is, indeed, true.

Merriam-Webster's Dictionary defines the word 'assume' this way: "To think that something is true or probably true without knowing that it is true."[43] For thousands of years, most people assumed the world was flat; they believed it possible to fall off the edge of the earth. They believed in the world's flatness as firmly as later generations would believe in its roundness.

Many people were brought up to believe that assumptions are bad; in many ways, however, assumptions are how we make sense of the world around us. For instance, we can't have 100 percent of the details of anything, so sometimes we must assume in order to make decisions. We are not 100 percent certain on anything, but sometimes we must take what we know and assume accordingly in order to make judgments.

Think of technology such as the smartphone and Facebook. This generation benefits from technology that allows human beings to be in contact with each other in a way previous generations couldn't have even imagined! Certainly, social media is beneficial in many ways, including for spreading the gospel. However, there are significant negative issues that have also developed with these modern means of communication.

One is the lack of what can be seen—body language is absent. When emailing, texting, or talking on the phone, there is no furrowing of eyebrows (unless you're using video chat technology). There are no visible smiles, frowns, or even tensing up of the body as can be seen in face-to-face communication. Texts and emails also eliminate voice tone and inflection. Does the person sound happy? Angry? Is their voice low or monotone?

Although we might try to alleviate such uncertainty by using emoji in our electronic communication, there is no way to truly understand how something was said without the use of body language or without the tone of the voice. In fact, one study out of *Psychology Today* has found that 55 percent of communication is with body language and 38 percent comes from the tone of voice. Only 7 percent of communication is derived from the actual words spoken.[44] So when two people text one another or communicate via Facebook, Instagram or Twitter, they are only communicating 7 percent!

The other 93 percent can't be seen or heard in the message. And lo and behold, this is where assumptions sneak in. "This is what a person must have meant," we think, based on what we think they meant from what we are *reading*.

Now, assumption isn't always bad—it can be good. But the problem is that people tend to assume the worst. It's human nature, as much a part of us as our DNA. Most people don't give others the benefit of the doubt on things. I know I have been guilty of this before! For instance, I've received a text message and immediately thought, "That sounds kind of rude!" Without that smiley face added on, or even an exclamation point, we unfairly conclude the person who sent the text is writing out of negative emotions.

Loving in the Midst of Assumptions

Christians, by contrast, are called to operate above the smiley-face level of communication. They are to show *agape* love even when what is being communicated seems like it's stemming from hurt, anger, bitterness, or pride, because God's love is not defined by humans—it's defined by God! The love that believers are to express to one another and to the world is God's love, and this love always assumes the best in others. This love is to be expressed even as we make assumptions of certain things—believers are always to consider the motives or actions of one another in a positive light.

Consider how Jesus Himself reacted to His suffering prior to His crucifixion:

A third time he said to them, "Why, what evil has he done? I have found in him no ground for the sentence of death; I will therefore have him flogged and then release him." But they kept urgently demanding with loud shouts that he should be crucified; and their voices prevailed. So Pilate gave his verdict that their demand should be granted. He released the man they asked for, the one who had been put in prison for insurrection and murder, and he handed Jesus over as they wished.

As they led him away, they seized a man, Simon of Cyrene, who was coming from the country, and they laid the cross on him, and made him carry it behind Jesus. A great number of the people followed him, and among them were women who were beating their breasts and wailing for him. But Jesus turned to them and said, "Daughters of Jerusalem, do not weep for me, but weep for yourselves and for your children. For the days are surely coming when they will say, 'Blessed are the barren, and the wombs that never bore, and the breasts that never nursed.' Then they will begin to say to the mountains, 'Fall on us'; and to the hills, 'Cover us.' For if they do this when the wood is green, what will happen when it is dry?"

Two others also, who were criminals, were led away to be put to death with him. When they came to the place that is called The Skull, they crucified Jesus there with the criminals, one on his right and one on his left. Then Jesus said, "Father, forgive them; for they do not know what they are doing." — Luke 23:22–34 (NRSV)

In the midst of such a dark and dreary scene, genuine *agape* love was manifested. With criminals on both sides of Him, soldiers gambling away His clothing beneath His bloodied feet (Luke 23:34), and loud voices mocking the Son of God (Luke 23:35–37), *agape* love was poured out. Though the crowd yelled, "Crucify Him!" and chose a murderer over an innocent man, though they nailed Jesus to a cross to execute Him between two criminals, Jesus saw through the darkness and these acts of selfishness and hatred—and asked His Father to forgive them.

Step into Jesus' sandals for a moment; consider where He was. If I went to the cross and heard the shouts of those who demanded my death, knowing I was innocent, knowing a murderer was given freedom while I was flogged and hung on a tree to die, I would have been angry in my soul at those soldiers as they gambled my clothes away.

Yet in this situation, Jesus' response is much different. Jesus asks the Father to forgive them for what they are doing. They don't know or understand the gravity of their sin. Unlike mere human beings, Jesus never has to assume the best in others; He already knows what's in a person's mind and heart.

While others hated tax collectors, who in Jesus' day were known to be corrupt, Jesus looked past their current state and saw who God intended them to be. He called one particular tax collector, Matthew, to follow Him as His disciple. Jesus saw fishermen, tax collectors, prostitutes, and so many others as children of God, righteous and redeemed because of Jesus' work on the cross—and He does the same for us!

When no one else in society will give a person a chance, Jesus gives them a chance. This is the love of Jesus, and this is the committed, selfless love, given without expecting anything in return, that believers are supposed to demonstrate toward one another and toward non-believers.

Agape Love Is Impossible—Without God

It's not easy to assume the best in people. In fact, it's near impossible! Scripture says that "all have sinned and fall short of the glory of God" (Romans 3:23 NIV). All people by nature are bent toward sin. Naturally, human beings are going to be compelled to operate out of human emotion. To be able to look past the sin, and look at the person for who they are to God—His child, His beloved—is only possible with God.

Matthew 5:46–47 says, "If you love only those who love you, what reward is there for that? Even corrupt tax collectors do that much. If you are kind only to your friends, how are you different from anyone else? Even pagans do that" (NLT). God calls His children to love beyond what is easy.

Tax collectors in Jesus' time were disloyal men who had been hired by the Romans to tax their Jewish brothers for personal profit. Because of this, Jews hated tax collectors. But Jesus says even these crooked tax collectors love their own kind! This is not *agape* love. *Agape* is not limited to those who love you; even sinners will do that. No, *agape* love surpasses this, and loves the unlovable—or even the enemy.

Beloved theologian Charles Spurgeon writes beautifully of what this kind of divine love looks like:

> Ours it is to persist in loving, even if men persist in enmity. We are to render blessing for cursing, prayers for persecutions. Even in the cases of cruel enemies, we are to do good to them, and pray for them. We are no longer enemies to any, but friends to all. We do not merely cease to hate, and then abide in a cold neutrality; but we love where hatred seemed inevitable. We bless where our old nature bids us curse, and we are active in doing good to those who deserve to receive evil from us. —**Charles Spurgeon**[45]

Jesus' model of love challenges the believer to dig deep within their soul to the hidden places only God sees and to ask: Am I loving as God loves me, or am I loving whom I want to love?

Just one verse later, Matthew reveals how Christians are to love in this way:

But you are to be perfect, even as your Father in heaven is perfect. — Matthew 5:48 (NLT)

Here again is one of those English words that demands a proper interpretation to prevent misunderstanding what God is saying.

The Greek word used in Matthew 5:48 is the word *teleios*. It doesn't mean to be without fault. *Teleios* means to be "brought to its end, to be finished, to be completed or to be fully grown."[46] The verb in this verse, 'are,' is *estin*. Notice that it is written in the present tense: being "complete" in Christ-like love and perfection is the present and continual goal of the Christian—a pursuit that never ends.[47]

Christians are not perfect, in the ideological sense of the word; no matter how hard they try, they can never bring themselves to a place of completeness. Only God can transform a person, "for it is God who works in you to will and to act in order to fulfill his good purpose" (Philippians 2:13 NIV). At the great day of salvation, God will finish the work He began in you (Philippians 1:6).

In Genesis 17:1, God told Abraham the same thing, saying, "I am God Almighty; walk before me faithfully and be blameless" (NIV). Here, the Hebrew word for blameless is *tamiym*, which means "complete, singlehearted, sincere, and wholly to the Lord."[48]

God's command to *agapao*-love others is a call to move toward maturity in Him, the process of being made "complete" in Him. To be perfected in our intentions toward one another is to love others through the transformational grace of God. God calls believers to progressively love others more and more as He loves. John MacArthur puts it this way:

> Because God is perfect, those who are truly his children will move on in the direction of his perfect standard. If you are stalled, or if you are slipping in the opposite direction, it is right that you examine yourself. Pursuing the standard of perfection does not mean we can never fail. It means that when we fail we deal with it ... a genuine believer will, as a pattern of life, be confessing sin and coming to the Father for forgiveness.[49]

When I teach this, I often hear, "But Pastor—you don't know what that person did to me! You don't know the history that we have with one another! You don't know the hurt that I have had to endure and the things that have been said behind my back!" True, when someone has been deeply scarred by hurt, it does seem near impossible to then love as God loves. Yet it is possible—because what God charges and requires of His children, He also makes possible to be accomplished by the power of the Holy Spirit dwelling within the believer.

This journey will not happen overnight; it is something God calls Christians to press on toward, because one day when we see Christ "we shall be like him" (1 John 3:2 NIV). Only then will we be wholly perfect—glorified fully into the image of the Son.

Paul understood this tension of wanting to love as God loves, but in his own strength not being able to love in the fullness of His love. He wrote, "I press on so that I may lay hold of that for which also I was laid hold of by Christ Jesus" (Philippians 3:12 NASB). Paul knew he was perfect before God in his position as a truly saved and sanctified follower of Christ, but also that he was being perfected while living out his present life on earth. So, too, are we.

Be Transformed in Mind and Heart

> A scuba diver lives in the water but breathes the air. He is able to function because he takes his environment with him. If he "conforms" to the environment around him, he will eventually die. —**Anonymous**[50]

Throughout both the Old and New Testaments, in numerous scriptures about loving God and others, He has directed us *not* to conform to the ways of the world. If you really want to act out His godly love toward people, a love that assumes the best in one another regardless of what is said or not said, regardless of what a text message seems to mean or how a person acts, *ask God for it*. Ask Him to transform your mind to give you Christ's mind—which Paul says the believer already has and thus can claim—so you can see people the way that God sees them: "For who has known the mind of the Lord so as to instruct him? But we have the mind of Christ" (1 Corinthians 2:16 NRSV).

In Romans 12:2 Paul writes to believers: "...not [to] be conformed to this world, but be transformed by the renewing of your minds, so that you may discern what is the will of God—what is good and acceptable and perfect" (NRSV). Another translation simplifies what Paul meant here: "Don't let the world around you squeeze you into its own mould [mold]" (PHILLIPS). Believers must live in the world that constantly tries to pull them away from God, yet not be "of" the world. This is the word 'conformed' in English; in the original Greek, however, it is the word *suschematizo*, meaning "to form according to a pattern or mold, to fashion alike, to conform to the same pattern outwardly."[51]

In Romans 12:2, then, what Paul says to press against is conformity to "this world," or what some translators call "the age"—the present, sinful age that "lies under the power of the evil one" (1 John 5:19 NRSV). After all, Satan is "the god of this world" (2 Corinthians 4:4 NRSV), so this present age is not what we want forming us!

Instead, believers are to resist and fight against the present age! Believers are to let God transform them into new people by changing the way they think. Then, as Paul said, "you may discern what is the will of God—what is good and acceptable and perfect" (Romans 12:2 NRSV). To be transformed means be shaped or changed into another form. It is derived from the word *metamorphoo*, from which the English word 'metamorphosis' comes. It is "an inward renewal of the mind" in which the believer's spirit "is changed into the likeness of Christ" and, ultimately, is reflected in their character and behavior on the outside.[52]

The mind is what controls a person's attitudes, feelings, actions, and thoughts. The more your mind is conformed to be like Christ's, the more your attitudes, feelings, actions, and thoughts will align with God's—including His attitude of love toward others. Do this by reading and meditating on the Word of God, concentrating on God's living and active word to you, which will pierce your heart and soul and be what does the transforming!

This concept of transformation was a common theme in Paul's letters. To the Corinthians he wrote, "But we all, with unveiled face, beholding as in a mirror the glory of the Lord, are being transformed into the same image from glory to glory, just as from the Lord, the Spirit" (2 Corinthians 3:18 NASB).

If you want to assume the best in others, ask God to give you the mind of Christ, to change your mind, and ultimately to transform your heart to love people the way He wants you to love—to express a love that assumes the best in others. It very much may be a daily struggle and a daily challenge, but *it is possible* with the empowerment of the Holy Spirit. If you struggle in finding love for a particular person, ask God to help you see that person through His eyes.

What's in a Name?

Our Father, we pray that we will more than just intellectually grasp this truth, but that it may grip our hearts and our souls, and release our paralyzed wills, and energize us to begin to be available to You, not in words but in deeds. —Ray Stedman[53]

Our God doesn't only love other people, of course—He also loves you—too much to leave you the way you came to Him. He wants you to experience life to the fullest! God is in the business of transforming lives. Consider Abram, an older man who had lived out seventy-

five years of his life when God approached him with a
great promise:

> *Now the LORD said to Abram, "Go from your country and*
> *your kindred and your father's house to the land that I*
> *will show you. I will make of you a great nation, and I will*
> *bless you, and make your name great, so that you will be*
> *a blessing. I will bless those who bless you, and the one*
> *who curses you I will curse; and in you all the families of*
> *the earth shall be blessed."* — **Genesis 12:1–3 (NRSV)**

God told Abram that He was going to make him into a
great nation, bless him, and make his name great. Later,
God said:

> *I will surely bless you and make your descendants as*
> *numerous as the stars in the sky and as the sand on the*
> *seashore. Your descendants will take possession of the*
> *cities of their enemies...* — **Genesis 22:17 (NIV)**

The only problem with this scenario is that Abram was
quite old, and his wife, Sarai, was well past childbearing
age! But God made a promise, and God is a covenant-
keeper. He had declared, "No longer shall your name be
Abram, but your name shall be Abraham; for I have made
you the ancestor of a multitude of nations. I will make you
exceedingly fruitful; and I will make nations of you, and
kings shall come from you" (Genesis 17:5–6 NRSV).

This change of names is not just an addition of a few
Hebrew letters. No, in ancient biblical times, a name
identified something about the nature of the person.

'Abram' in Hebrew means "father of height." However, 'Abraham' means "father of a multitude."[54] God was changing Abraham's name to what God intended him to be!

Later in the biblical narrative, God caused Sarai (whose name He changed from Sarai, meaning "princess," to Sarah, meaning "chieftainess"[55]) to become pregnant with Isaac, from whose son Jacob would come the twelve tribes of Israel. God kept His word to Abraham: though Abraham didn't see the fulfillment of God's word that he would be the father of a "multitude of nations," God remained true to His word.

In the New Testament, this same activity of changing names occurs. God changed Simon's name to Peter. Simon's name, which derived from the word 'hearing,'[56] changed to Peter, meaning "Rock." On the day of Pentecost, it was Peter who preached, and thousands came to Jesus Christ (Acts 2:14–42). Peter lived up to his name, God's new mission for him in life. Jesus speaks to who Peter *would* be.

You are not what others think you are. You are what God knows you are. — **Shannon L. Alder**[57]

This is just like God, who is in the business of transforming people and does so out of the overflow of His nature, which is *agape* love.

Unfortunately, people often come to God but only dabble in His love, so they do not receive the fullness that He offeres. A good analogy would be a father who provides a car to his sixteen-year-old son. The father parks the car in the driveway, walks inside the house, and hands his son the keys—but the son says, "Thanks, Dad!" and remains on the couch, watching TV. The gift has been given, but not received—and the son doesn't experience the fullness of joy that comes from the gift!

Many also believe the lie that they will never—or can never—be changed. They think they will stay the way they are, forever. "This is just how I am," they think. However, this is not what God says.

Paul, writing to the Philippian church, addresses this issue: "I am confident of this, that the one who began a good work among you will bring it to completion by the day of Jesus Christ" (Philippians 1:6 NRSV).

God is not finished with you, me, or anyone who puts their faith in Jesus. God began the good work, and He promises He "will bring it to completion," or fullness. However, there is commitment on the believer's part. Later, in Philippians 2:12–13, Paul directed believers to "work out your own salvation with fear and trembling, for it is God who works in you to will and to act in order to fulfill his good purpose" (NIV). God works in the believer, enabling him or her both to be changed and to carry out the work God intends. It is a lifelong process, and one that won't come to perfect completion until heaven. No one has "arrived."

Yet God is waiting to give you a fullness of life only possible by the indwelling power of the Holy Spirit. Are you fully allowing God to love you? Or are you refusing His love by the way that you see yourself? Are you turning down the gift, which is waiting for you like the teen's car in the driveway? God wants people restored to His image.

In Genesis, God created man and woman, and they walked in His presence in the garden. They were not ashamed. When God created them, He said, "Let us make man in our image, according to our likeness" (Genesis 1:26 ESV).

This was God's intention from the beginning—to create a people who reflected His image and who would draw other people and nations to Himself. Today, God's desire is that the church would reflect that image. Colossians 1:15 says that Jesus is "the image of the invisible God, the firstborn over all creation" (NIV), and Hebrews 1:3 says Jesus is "the radiance of God's glory and the exact representation of his being" (NIV).

To manifest God's *agape* love, then, the believer need only look to Jesus, the author and completer of faith, to see what *agape* love looks like. This is why Paul was able to tell his followers, "And you should imitate me, just as I imitate Christ" (1 Corinthians 11:1 NLT).

Paul called the Corinthian church to imitate him and how he loved others, as Paul imitated Christ. The result? More and more believers who "look" like Jesus—who express sacrificial, committed, selfless love to a lost world.

Chapter 5 Questions

Question: How, being as specific as you can, has Christ transformed your heart and your life?

_____

_____

_____

_____

_____

_____

_____

_____

_____

_____

_____

Question: What do you think God might name you? That is, if your name were to reflect your relationship with God, what would it be?

_____

_____

_____

_____

_____

_____

_____

_____

_____

_____

_____

_____

Action: Rise above a life based on assumptions and offense, and instead reflect the selfless love of Christ at all times. Immerse yourself in the Word and pray continuously so that God's *agape* love might gradually conform every detail of your life to the model of Christ!

Chapter 5 Notes

CHAPTER SIX

Guard the Flock

Lynn Anderson, in *They Smell Like Sheep*, relates this story:

Several years ago in Palestine, Carolyn and I rode a tour bus through Israel's countryside nearly mesmerized as the tour guide explained the scenery, the history, and the lifestyle. In his description, he included a heart-warming portrayal of the ancient shepherd/sheep relationship. He expounded on how the shepherd builds a relationship with his sheep—how he feeds them and gently cares for them. He pointed out that the shepherd doesn't drive the sheep but leads them, and that the shepherd does not need to be harsh with them, because they hear his voice and follow. And so on ... He then explained how on a previous tour things had backfired for him as he was giving this same speech about sheep and shepherds. In the midst of spinning his pastoral tale, he suddenly realized he had lost his audience. They were all staring out the bus window at a guy chasing a 'herd' of sheep. He was throwing rocks at them, whacking them with sticks, and sic'ing the sheep dog on them. The sheep-driving man in the field had torpedoed the guide's enchanting narrative. The guide told us that he had been so agitated that he jumped off the bus, ran into the field, and accosted the man, "Do you understand what you have just done to me?" he asked. "I was spinning a charming story about the gentle ways of shepherds, and here you are mistreating, hazing, and assaulting these sheep What is going on?" For a moment, a bewildered look froze on the face of the poor sheep-chaser, then the light dawned and he blurted out, "Man. You've got me all wrong. I'm not a shepherd. I'm a butcher." This poor unwitting fellow had just provided the tour guide and all of us with a perfect example of what a "good shepherd" is not.[58]

Woven throughout the pages of Scripture is the tender motif of a shepherd. As ambassadors of Christ who are called to love as God loves, we are to guard the flocks He has entrusted to us, too. Though some may think that the concept of "shepherding" only applies to clergy, the truth is that godly love (a love that all Christians are expected to exhibit) is one that protects and one that provides life. As people of God, we are all called to act out a love that protects others and a love that provides life to others—as a shepherd lays down his life so that the sheep might live.

While the thought of loving like a shepherd might seem simple enough, we are reminded that God issued strong rebukes for bad shepherds while foretelling of a good shepherd to come—manifested in the person of Jesus Christ, who identified Himself as *the* Good Shepherd and His role as guarding His tender flock.

Characteristics of a Good Shepherd

First, however, let's look at what the Bible says about *bad* shepherds. Ezekiel wrote that ancient Israel's leaders, who were supposed to be shepherding God's people, had failed miserably, in a sense slaughtering their sheep for personal benefit rather than tending them and feeding them. Ezekiel says these leaders treated God's people with force and harshness:

> The word of the LORD came to me: Mortal, prophesy against the shepherds of Israel: prophesy, and say to them—to the shepherds: Thus says the Lord GOD: Ah, you shepherds of Israel who have been feeding yourselves! Should not shepherds feed the sheep? You eat the fat, you clothe yourselves with the wool, you slaughter the fatlings; but you do not feed the sheep. You have not strengthened the weak, you have not healed the sick, you have not bound up the injured, you have not brought back the strayed, you have not sought the lost, but with force and harshness you have ruled them. — *Ezekiel 34:1–4 (NRSV)*

Jeremiah echoes this, saying that the shepherds had "become stupid and have not sought the LORD; therefore they have not prospered, and all their flock is scattered" (Jeremiah 10:21 NASB). Because of bad shepherding, the people of Israel fell away from God, followed their own selfish ambitions, and disregarded God's instruction. As a result, God allowed for Israel to be scattered to the four corners of the earth.

Conversely, Scripture also identifies "good shepherds," those individuals of God who cared for God's flock well. The most famous is David. Psalm 78:70–72 says:

He chose his servant David, and took him from the sheepfolds; from tending the nursing ewes he brought him to be the shepherd of his people Jacob, of Israel, his inheritance. With upright heart he tended them, and guided them with skillful hand. (NRSV)

Shepherds cared for the flock, guided and provided for their sheep, and led them to green pastures for food and to streams for water. They protected their sheep and kept them safe. If the sheep's lives were in danger because of a wild animal or a robber, the shepherd would risk his own to save even one sheep. The shepherd was close with each individual sheep, so much so that they knew his voice when he called—recognizing the distinct tone of the shepherd's voice.

King David understood God to be his divine shepherd:

The Lord is my shepherd, I shall not want. He makes me lie down in green pastures; he leads me beside still waters; he restores my soul. He leads me in right paths for his name's sake. Even though I walk through the darkest valley, I fear no evil; for you are with me; your rod and your staff—they comfort me. You prepare a table before me in the presence of my enemies; you anoint my head with oil; my cup overflows. Surely goodness and mercy shall follow me all the days of my life, and I shall dwell in the house of the Lord my whole life long.
— Psalm 23:1-6 (NRSV)

David's shepherd provided rest and restoration for his soul. He walked with David through dark valleys, and the shepherd's "rod and staff" truly comforted him. The nation of Israel knew God to be her Shepherd, the One who would provide for the nation and protect her.

In the New Testament, Jesus too would draw on the imagery of the shepherd and his flock—terms His Jewish listeners would have immediately understood:

> *Jesus used this figure of speech with them, but they did not understand what he was saying to them.*
>
> *So again Jesus said to them, "Very truly, I tell you, I am the gate for the sheep. All who came before me are thieves and bandits; but the sheep did not listen to them. I am the gate. Whoever enters by me will be saved, and will come in and go out and find pasture. The thief comes only to steal and kill and destroy. I came that they may have life, and have it abundantly.*
>
> *I am the good shepherd. The good shepherd lays down his life for the sheep. The hired hand, who is not the shepherd and does not own the sheep, sees the wolf coming and leaves the sheep and runs away—and the wolf snatches them and scatters them. The hired hand runs away because a hired hand does not care for the sheep. I am the good shepherd. I know my own and my own know me, just as the Father knows me and I know the Father. And I lay down my life for the sheep. I have other sheep that do not belong to this fold. I must bring them also, and they will listen to my voice. So there will be one flock, one shepherd. For this reason the Father loves me, because I lay down my life in order to take it up again. No one takes it from me, but I lay it down of my own accord. I have power to lay it down, and I have power to take it up again. I have received this command from my Father." — John 10:6–18 (NRSV)*

When Jesus cast Himself as this good shepherd, Jews who were listening would have known exactly what He was saying: Jesus was placing Himself in the position of God—the One they knew to be the Good Shepherd. Essentially, Jesus was proclaiming, "There is only one shepherd and that's Me! There is only one flock and that's My flock!" By claiming to be the Good Shepherd, Jesus was claiming deity.

The true Good Shepherd is sacrificial—willing to cast aside His own needs for the needs of the sheep, or God's children. This is why Jesus continually spoke of a shepherd giving his own life for the sheep.

In this, Jesus is being clear that there is no other way to be a part of the flock than to follow Jesus as a sheep follows its shepherd. Furthermore, in John 10:10, Jesus clarified the distinction between Himself and the enemy: the enemy's goal is to steal, kill, destroy, and create disunity and distraction. His purpose is to lead people to falsehood, to speak lies into their hearts and minds, and to lure their eyes off of the true Shepherd.

By contrast, Jesus said, "I have come that they may have life, and have it to the full" (John 10:10 NIV). In the Greek, the word 'full' indicates an everlasting life, a fullness of life—what it really means to follow God, what it really means to embrace the love that He has for those who love Him. And thus, life results from love. Think of creation, which took place because God wanted to express His love. He created human beings in His image; we are "fearfully and wonderfully made," according to Psalm 139:14 (NRSV). That's God's love for you: life results from His love.

Finally, the prophet Isaiah wrote that the Good Shepherd will feed His flock: "He will feed his flock like a shepherd; he will gather the lambs in his arms, and carry them in his bosom, and gently lead the mother sheep" (Isaiah 40:11 NRSV). To "feed," in the original Hebrew, means "to pasture, tend, [or] graze."[59]

But one definition of 'feeding' is most striking: "to keep company" or "associate with (as a friend)."[60] There is something divinely beautiful and intimate about this imagery of a shepherd feeding his flock; God is taking care of His people as a close, special friend.

> God has entrusted us with his most precious treasure - people. He asks us to shepherd and mold them into strong disciples, with brave faith and good character.
> — John Ortberg[61]

I remember when my wife and I first learned we were having Melissa. To be honest, Melissa was life-giving in many ways. There were many frustrating things we were having to deal with at that time—some of them in ministry, some of them in life. We needed to know God's protection, provision and love for us. Then, we found out that we were pregnant with Melissa.

I remember that first moment we heard Melissa's heartbeat at the doctor's office and it took my breath away. I was hearing life that resulted from a love I shared with my wife. I was overwhelmed. This is God's design— that life be the byproduct of love. This is what Jesus meant when He said He came that we might have life to the fullest. He wants to love us in a way greater than we can ever comprehend.

Real *agape* love isn't about a shallow, partially full life; it is about a full life. Think about parenting. Most parents want the best for their kids and would do anything for them—even sacrifice their own life for their child. This parental love does not even come close to comparing to the love that God has for us. Even the best parents cannot love with the fullness that God loves.

And yet, this is what God calls believers to—He has an expectation for us to love others in a way that far exceeds anything a person could ever imagine or comprehend.

Priest and author Joseph Langford once wrote, "The same God who loves us as we are also loves us too much to leave us as we are."[62] God wants His children to experience fullness of life.

Keep Watch over the Flock

Keep watch over yourselves and over all the flock, of which the Holy Spirit has made you overseers, to shepherd the church of God that he obtained with the blood of his own Son. — Acts 20:28 (NRSV)

Let's continue examining this concept of Jesus as the divine Good Shepherd who cares for, protects, and provides for His flock. In Acts 20:28, Paul now exhorts the church, "Keep watch ... over all the flock" (NRSV).

An alternative translation is "Be on guard" (Acts 20:28 NASB). Paul was firmly instructing the believers to beware or pay attention to, or "keep a watchful eye on," the flock of Christ. This is the Greek word *prosecho*, which literally means "to hold the mind" toward someone or something.[63] In a figurative sense, to "be on guard" is a command to be on continual lookout for those agents of Satan who sneak in to destroy God's church.

Accordingly, in Acts 20:29, Paul said, "I know that after my departure savage wolves will come in among you, not sparing the flock" (NASB). Paul was deeply intentional in choosing the phrase "savage wolves." For a sheepfold, a wolf is the greatest enemy because it causes great destruction; for the church, the greatest enemies are Satan and his spiritual wolves who "disguise themselves as ministers of righteousness" (2 Corinthians 11:14–15 NRSV).

Thus, God instructs Christians to guard their own hearts aggressively, but also to guard the hearts of other believers who may be deceived. Paul said that believers are to guard "all the flock"—the whole church—not some of the flock. The writer of Proverbs used a similar Hebrew word, instructing, "Watch over your heart with all diligence" (Proverbs 4:23 NASB).

Jesus Christ is the Great Shepherd over the entire church, the *ekklesia*, God's "called out ones."[64] But God has made believers "overseers" of the flock, representing Christ—enabled to do His work of protecting, guarding, providing for, and tending, by the power of the Holy Spirit.

Don't miss the beauty of what an "overseer" was intended to be. 'Overseer' is a word that comes from the Greek word *episkopos*,[65] from *epi* ("over or upon") and *skopos* ("goal or end in view")[66]. Consider the word 'telescope' and note the root word *skopos* within it. What function does a telescope have? To bring something far off into closer vision. An overseer, therefore, is one who looks over God's people closely or intently, viewing them carefully and watching over them in Christ's place.

In Paul's day, he called the new believers in Jesus to step in and be overseers of the church. Believers today have that same calling:

> A shepherd guides and guards his sheep, grooming them, going before them, leading them beside still waters and green pastures. He knows each one by name. He fends for them, fights for them, feeds them, gathers them into the fold. The Lord Jesus portrayed Himself as a Shepherd. Paul reminds these elders that they are under-shepherds of "the church of God, which he hath purchased with his own blood." Purchased at such cost, the Lord's people are of infinite worth, and the work of a shepherd one of awesome responsibility. —John Phillips[67]

Protection from the "Wolves"

For overseers trying to protect the church from deceivers, the fairy tale of Little Red Riding Hood proves instructive. You probably know the story already: Little Red Riding Hood went on a journey to visit her grandma, and encountered a terrible wolf. The bad wolf disguised himself to look like Grandma—lying in her bed, prepared to eat Little Red Riding Hood upon her arrival.

And the bad wolf almost dined on Little Red Riding Hood, who was not able to tell—despite the hairy chin and big fangs—that this was not, in fact, Grandma in the bed. Red's discernment skills were clearly not up to par.

Many times, the church's ability to discern truth from error is likewise subpar. God's enemies are intent on destroying the church. Like the wolf in grandma's clothing, they prey on the flock of God, deceiving those who have not guarded themselves with truth. Sometimes, sadly, these "wolves" will even use the Word of God against the church—using it to deceive! It is paramount that the church stand up and defend itself. God's sheep must know the truth, speak the truth, and fight for the truth, even in the face of spiritual wolves!

Paul exhorted believers, "Be of sober spirit, be on the alert. Your adversary, the devil, prowls around like a roaring lion, seeking someone to devour" (1 Peter 5:8 NASB). And John writes in John 10:12, "The hired hand, who is not the shepherd and does not own the sheep, sees the wolf coming and leaves the sheep and runs away— and the wolf snatches them and scatters them" (NRSV).

Make note of the wolves' actions: wolves snatch and scatter the sheep, or God's children. "Wolves" in Scripture are false teachers, who speak about corrupt or perverse things. Thus, Acts 20:30 says that "from among your own selves men will arise, speaking perverse things, to draw away the disciples after them" (NASB). From among the very people who call themselves followers of Christ—from the inside—the enemy will do great damage. He will mislead many with deceitful instruction.

The only way to guard the flock against the wolves— those false teachers with evil intent—is with the Word of God. How can believers take action against wolves whose intent is to divide and scatter God's sheep? They must study, meditate on and know God's Word, and listen to

Him, in order to prevent themselves and others from being swept away by error.

Proverbs 30:5 says, "Every word of God proves true. He is a shield to all who come to him for protection" (NLT). God's Word is a shield of protection. Paul borrowed this imagery as he instructed believers, "Put on the whole armor of God, so that you may be able to stand against the wiles of the devil" (Ephesians 6:11 NRSV). And after a long list of defensive armor, Paul told believers to take up the "sword of the Spirit, which is the word of God":

> *Above all, taking the shield of faith, wherewith ye shall be able to quench all the fiery darts of the wicked. And take the helmet of salvation, and the sword of the Spirit, which is the word of God.* — **Ephesians 6:16–17 (KJV)**

In biblical times, Romans used a short, double-edged sword known as a *gladius*.[68] Shields and helmets protected the soldier, but a sword was for both offensive and defensive purposes.

This "sword" of the Spirit is powerful and effective. The writer of Hebrews says that "the word of God is living and active, sharper than any two-edged sword, piercing until it divides soul from spirit, joints from marrow; it is able to judge the thoughts and intentions of the heart" (Hebrews 4:12 NRSV). The Word of God searches man's hearts, prepares people for spiritual battle against the enemy, helps believers discern truth from error, and also brings comfort. Notice what the psalmist said regarding the Word of God:

I treasure your word in my heart, so that I may not sin against you. — **Psalm 119:11 (NRSV)**

The psalmist, likely King David, knew that it was the Word of God alone that would keep him from falling to the wiles of the enemy. In the same way, the Word of God is a shield and a sword for the believer. As overseers of the flock, the church has a great responsibility to be feeding God's people truth, only found in the Word of God. It is this truth, and this truth alone that will "guard the flock."

Love Gives Life

And so it is written, The first man Adam was made a living soul; the last Adam was made a quickening spirit. — **1 Corinthians 15:45 (KJV)**

When we guard ourselves and the flock from falsehood, and instead cling to God's Word, love incarnate—that is, Jesus—becomes a life-giving Spirit within us. Paul wrote in 1 Corinthians 15:45 that Christ in the believer regenerates or "renews" them. There is a new pattern, a new template for love; thus, the believer is created according to the template of the Holy Spirit, as Paul says:

And all of us, with unveiled faces, seeing the glory of the Lord as though reflected in a mirror, are being transformed into the same image from one degree of

glory to another; for this comes from the Lord, the Spirit.
— *2 Corinthians 3:18 (NRSV)*

We behold the glory of the Lord Jesus and are transformed into that glory by the Lord Jesus, who is the Spirit. This occurs after a person is redeemed and changed. And the Spirit is Jesus' acting presence among His flock, producing His image among the body—His desires, His likeness, and His *agape* love.

WORKBOOK

Chapter 6 Questions

Question: Who in God's flock can you help tend for Jesus? What are some ways in which can you protect them, and feed them His love and truth?

_____

_____

_____

_____

_____

_____

_____

_____

_____

_____

_____

Question: How can recognize deceivers? What are some practical ways you can use the shield of faith and the sword of the Word against deception?

Action: Accept Christ as your Good Shepherd, and let His selflessly protective love pour through you into others! Find ways to act as an overseer, helping to tend His flock in your home and especially in the church. In doing so, be on the lookout for spiritual wolves! Look to the Word and the Spirit to help you identify and lovingly defend the flock, including yourself, against false teachers and their deceptions.

Chapter 6 Notes

_____

_____

_____

_____

_____

_____

_____

_____

_____

_____

_____

_____

_____

_____

_____

_____

_____

_____

_____

_____

_____

_____

_____

CONCLUSION

Unfailing Love

Love never fails. — *1 Corinthians 13:8 (NIV)*

Mother Teresa once wrote, "I'm a little pencil in the hand of a writing God, who is sending a love letter to the world."[69]

God is calling the church today to a higher place—one that expresses His very nature to a world deceived, lost, hopeless, and bleeding. God is calling the church to be part of that "love letter" to the world. It is a calling to the highest level of love: committed, sacrificial, *agape* love. This is a love that puts others first, sacrifices for others, and gives up personal rights. It is a love that loves without condition, and loves humbly without any expectation of that love being returned.

God's love transcends human understanding, and can only be expressed by the One from whom it originates: Jesus Christ, God in the flesh. Do you know the source of this love? Do you know Jesus, your Savior?

Those who believe in Jesus have the Spirit of God within them. Isn't that hard to comprehend? God, who in His character is *agape* love, lives within mere human beings! This gift of grace is present; believers need only take hold of the gift and allow God to do the work of loving others.

Dieter F. Uchtdorf wrote of God's love, "Though we are incomplete, God loves us completely. Though we are imperfect, He loves us perfectly. Though we may feel lost and without compass, God's love encompasses us completely. He loves every one of us, even those who are flawed, rejected, awkward, sorrowful, or broken."[70]

However, loving others as God loves us is not easy; it takes a willingness to be humble before God and allow Him to transform hearts that are stubborn, selfish, and drawn toward worldly things into hearts fully committed to Him. For those who are willing, God is ready to change their very nature to be more like His. He will take those stubborn hearts and gently and slowly mold them to love even the most difficult people in their lives.

Isaiah, speaking for God, declared, "'My thoughts are nothing like your thoughts,' says the LORD. 'And my ways are far beyond anything you could imagine'" (Isaiah 55:8 NLT). And yet Paul said, "For, 'Who can know the LORD's thoughts? Who knows enough to teach him?' But we understand these things, for we have the mind of Christ" (1 Corinthians 2:16 NLT). Those who believe in Jesus, who indwells them, are supernaturally enabled to be in alignment with the thoughts, the mind, and the heart of God!

Take up the charge to reflect Jesus to the world. Your commitment to come before God as a servant, willing to be used by God however He deems necessary, is a soothing aroma to Him—a pleasing sacrifice. It will not be an easy road, but it will be a journey that God promises will bring a fullness to life that the world cannot offer. It will be a taste of heaven on earth! When we love as Jesus loves, part of God's Kingdom is established upon the earth.

The Good Shepherd is watching and guarding His flock—loving them perfectly—and He is asking for people devoted to Him to join Him in participating in the job: "The eyes of the LORD search the whole earth in order to strengthen those whose hearts are fully committed to him" (2 Chronicles 16:9 NLT). Are you ready to take on this awesome responsibility?

In the midst of this amazing privilege, God promises that He will never leave you or forsake you. He will be intimately a part of what He is calling you to do. His *agape* love will fill you to overflowing so that you are able, in turn, to love others the same way. *He will help you*!

Remember that this journey is not about who you are now, or even who you think you are. It is a progressive walk with the Lord, who takes those sheep who are close to His heels and transforms them to be what He already has created and planned for them to be.

As Stormie Omartian wrote in her book *The Power of a Praying Woman*, "It's not about finding ways to avoid God's judgment and feeling like a failure if you don't do everything perfectly. It's about fully experiencing God's love and letting it perfect you. It's not about being somebody you are not. It's about becoming who you really are."[71]

This is God's perfect love for you and for the world. And this love will never fail.

REFERENCES

Notes

1. Lennon, John. "All You Need Is Love" (song lyrics). 1967. In *AZLyrics*. http://www.azlyrics.com/lyrics/beatles/allyouneedislove.html
2. Spindel, Carly. "What Does Love Mean?" *Huffington Post*. http://www.huffingtonpost.com/carly-spindel/what-does-love-mean_b_7801880.html 7/16/15
3. "Love." *Merriam-Webster*. https://www.merriam-webster.com/dictionary/love
4. Poe, Edgar Allan. "Annabel Lee." In *Poetry Foundation*. https://www.poetryfoundation.org/poems-and-poets/poems/detail/44885
5. "How Many Words Are There in the Greek Language for Love?" *Never Thirsty*. Like the Master Ministries. https://www.neverthirsty.org/bible-qa/qa-

archives/question/how-many-words-are-there-in-the-greek-language-for-love/

6. *Ibid.*

7. "5387. philostorgos." From *Thayer's Greek Lexicon*, Electronic Database. Biblesoft, Inc., 2011. *Bible Hub.* http://biblehub.com/str/greek/5387.htm

8. "5360. phileo." From *Thayer's Expanded Greek Definition*, Electronic Database. Biblesoft, Inc., 2011. *Study Light.* http://www.studylight.org/lexicons/greek/gwview.cgi?n=5360

9. "157. aheb." *Bible Hub.* http://biblehub.com/hebrew/157.htm

10. Wellman, Jack. "What Is Agape Love?" From *Christian Crier*, Telling Ministries. *Patheos.* 2 May 2014. http://www.patheos.com/blogs/christiancrier/2014/05/02/what-is-agape-love-a-bible-study/

11. "25. agapaó." *Bible Hub.* http://biblehub.com/greek/25.htm

12. Bloesch, D. G. *God, the Almighty: Power, Wisdom, Holiness, Love.* InterVarsity Press, 2006, p. 145.

13. Bruce, F. F. *Christian Quotes.* http://www.christianquotes.info/images/f-f-bruce-quote-7-truths-gods-encompassing-love-blessing/

14. Nelmes, David. "God Is Agape Love." *Being Willing.* http://www.beingwilling.com/articles/god-agape-love.html 9/11/2007

15. Fowler, James A. "Push-ups." http://christinyou.net/pages/pushups.html c2004
16. "2175. euodia." From *Thayer's Greek Lexicon*, Electronic Database. Biblesoft, Inc., 2011. *Bible Hub*. http://biblehub.com/greek/2175.htm
17. Cartwright, Mark. "Roman Triumph." *Ancient History Encyclopedia*, 2016. http://www.ancient.eu/Roman_Triumph/
18. Meyer, F. B. "Ephesians 6 – Love: On God's Side." In *oChristian.com*. http://articles.ochristian.com/article11768.shtml
19. Teresa, Mother. In "Mother Teresa > Quotes > Quotable Quote." *Goodreads*. Goodreads Inc. http://www.goodreads.com/quotes/6303-i-am-not-sure-exactly-what-heaven-will-be-like
20. "3114. makrothymeō." From *Thayer's Expanded Greek Definition*, Electronic Database. Biblesoft, Inc., 2011. *Study Light*. http://www.studylight.org/lexicons/greek/gwview.cgi?n=3114
21. "5544. chréstotés." From *Thayer's Greek Lexicon*, Electronic Database. Biblesoft, Inc., 2011. *Bible Hub*. http://biblehub.com/greek/5544.htm
22. "2206. zēloō." From *Thayer's Greek Lexicon*, Electronic Database. Biblesoft, Inc., 2011. *Bible Hub*. http://biblehub.com/greek/2206.htm
23. Lewis, C. S. In "C. S. Lewis > Quotes > Quotable Quote." *Goodreads*. Goodreads Inc. http://www.goodreads.com/quotes/9707-a-proud-man-is-always-looking-down-on-things-and

24. "Arrogant." *Merriam-Webster.* https://www.merriam-webster.com/dictionary/arrogant

25. "807. aschēmoneō." From *NAS Exhaustive Concordance of the Bible with Hebrew-Aramaic and Greek Dictionaries.* The Lockman Foundation, 1998. *Bible Hub.* http://biblehub.com/greek/807.htm

26. Grant, Dawn. "Qualities You Display vs Qualities You Possess: Making Sense of Relationship Reality." *Dawn Grant.* 22 Feb. 2014. https://dawngrant.com/qualities-you-display-vs-qualities-you-possess-making-sense-of-relationship-reality/

27. Eliot, T. S. In "T. S. Eliot > Quotes > Quotable Quote." *Goodreads.* Goodreads Inc. http://www.goodreads.com/quotes/101806-half-the-harm-that-is-done-in-this-world-is

28. Hyde, Daniel. "The Word of God: How Am I to Love God by Loving It?" *Ligonier Ministries.* http://www.ligonier.org/blog/word-god-how-am-i-love-god-loving-it/ January 6, 2014

29. Chambers, Oswald. "9 Quotes About Restoration." *Christian Quotes.* http://www.christianquotes.info/quotes-by-topic/quotes-about-restoration/

30. Broger, John C. "9 Quotes About Restoration." *Christian Quotes.* http://www.christianquotes.info/quotes-by-topic/quotes-about-restoration/

31. Owen, John. "The Father's Discipline" *Ligonier Ministries.* http://www.ligonier.org/learn/devotionals/fathers-discipline/
32. Bolton, Brian. "Philip Yancey Tells about an African Safari He..." 11 May 2006. *Sermon Central.* Outreach, Inc. http://www.sermoncentral.com/illustrations/serm on-illustration-brian-bolton-quotes-27636
33. Lewis, C. S. *Mere Christianity.* HarperCollins Publishers, 1952.
34. "4768. stugnazó." From *Thayer's Greek Lexicon,* Electronic Database. Biblesoft, Inc., 2011. *Bible Hub.* http://biblehub.com/greek/4768.htm
35. "Mark 10:21." *Bible Hub.* http://biblehub.com/lexicon/mark/10-21.htm
36. MacArthur, John. *1 Corinthians* (The MacArthur New Testament Commentary). Moody, 1984, p. 132.
37. Charnock, Stephen. "Stephen Charnock Quotes." *Christian Quotes.* http://christian-quotes.ochristian.com/Stephen-Charnock-Quotes/
38. Carr, Alan. "Matthew 7:13–14: Where Will You End Up?" *Sermon Notebook.* http://www.sermonnotebook.org/new%20testame nt/matt%207_13-14.htm
39. "4439. pylē." From *Thayer's Expanded Greek Definition,* Electronic Database. Biblesoft, Inc., 2011. *Study Light.* http://www.studylight.org/lexicons/greek/gwview.cgi?n=4439
40. "Matthew 7:13–14 Commentary." *Precept Austin.* http://www.preceptaustin.org/matthew_713-14

41. *Ibid.*
42. Snicket, Lemony. *Austere Academy.* HarperCollins, 2000.
43. "Assume." *Merriam-Webster.* https://www.merriam-webster.com/dictionary/assume
44. Thompson, Jeff. "Is Nonverbal Communication a Numbers Game?" *Psychology Today.* https://www.psychologytoday.com/blog/beyond-words/201109/is-nonverbal-communication-numbers-game
45. Spurgeon, Charles. In "Spurgeon Exposition on Matthew 5:43-48." *APIBS.* Asia-Pacific Institute of Biblical Studies. http://www.apibs.info/bible-study/spurgeon/Matthew-5-43-TO-48.htm
46. "5046. teleios." From *Thayer's Greek Lexicon,* Electronic Database. Biblesoft, Inc., 2011. *Bible Hub.* http://biblehub.com/greek/5046.htm
47. "2076. esti." From *Thayer's Greek Lexicon,* Electronic Database. Biblesoft, Inc., 2011. *Bible Hub.* http://biblehub.com/greek/2076.htm
48. "Matthew 5:48 Commentary." *Precept Austin.* http://www.preceptaustin.org/matthew_548_be_perfect
49. *Ibid.*
50. "World – Kosmos (Greek Word Study)." *Precept Austin.* http://www.preceptaustin.org/index.php/node/61726
51. "4964. suschematizo." From *NAS Exhaustive Concordance of the Bible with Hebrew-Aramaic and Greek Dictionaries.* The Lockman

Foundation, 1998. Bible Hub. http://biblehub.com/greek/4964.htm

52. "2 Corinthians 3:18 Commentary." *Precept Austin.* http://www.preceptaustin.org/ 2corinthians_318_commentary

53. Stedman, Ray C. "Discovering the Will of God." *Ray Stedman.* http://www.raystedman.org/romans1/0023.html c2009

54. "All the Men of the Bible—Abram, Abraham." From *All the Men of the Bible*, Zondervan, 1988. *Bible Gateway.* https://www.biblegateway.com/ resources/all-men-bible/Abram-Abraham

55. "All the Women of the Bible—Sarah-Sarai-Sara." From *All the Women of the Bible.* Zondervan, 1988. *Bible Gateway.* https://www.biblegateway.com/resources/all-women-bible/Sarah-Sarai-Sara

56. "Simeon." *Bible Study Tools.* http://www.biblestudytools.com/dictionary/simeon/

57. Alder, Shannon L. "Shannon L. Alder > Quotes." *Goodreads.* Goodreads Inc. http://www.goodreads.com/author/quotes/1391130.Shannon_L_Alder

58. Anderson, Lynn. *They Smell Like Sheep: Spiritual Leadership for the 21st Century.* Howard Books, 2002.

59. "7462. ra'ah." From *Brown-Driver-Briggs Hebrew and English Lexicon* (Unabridged),

Electronic Database. Biblesoft, 2006. *Bible Hub.*
http://biblehub.com/hebrew/7462.htm

60. "7462. ra'ah." From *Strong's Exhaustive Concordance. Bible Hub.* http://biblehub.com/hebrew/7462.htm

61. Ortberg, John. "No More Mr. Nice Group." *Christianity Today.* http://www.christianitytoday.com/biblestudies/articles/spiritualformation/070704.html

62. Langford, Joseph. In "Joseph Langford." *Goodreads.* Goodreads Inc. https://www.goodreads.com/author/show/838639.Joseph_Langford

63. "4337. presechó." From *Strong's Exhaustive Concordance. Bible Hub.* http://biblehub.com/greek/4337.htm

64. Sproul, R. C. "Ekklesia; The Called-Out Ones." *Ligonier Ministries.* http://www.ligonier.org/blog/ekklesia-called-out-ones/

65. "1985. episkopos." From *NAS Exhaustive Concordance of the Bible with Hebrew-Aramaic and Greek Dictionaries.* The Lockman Foundation, 1998. *Bible Hub.* http://biblehub.com/greek/1985.htm

66. "4649. skopos." From *Thayer's Greek Lexicon,* Electronic Database. Biblesoft, 2011. *Bible Hub.* http://biblehub.com/greek/4649.htm

67. "Acts 20:28–38 Commentary." *Precept Austin.* http://www.preceptaustin.org/acts_2028-38_commentary

68. Grant, Michael. "The Roman Military in the New Testament." From *The Army of the Caesars*, Scribners, 1974. *Bible.org*. https://bible.org/article/roman-military-new-testament

69. Teresa, Mother. "Mother Teresa > Quotes > Quotable Quote." *Goodreads*. Goodreads Inc. http://www.goodreads.com/quotes/30608-i-m-a-little-pencil-in-the-hand-of-a-writing

70. Uchtdort, Dieter F. "Dieter F. Uchtdorf > Quotes." *Goodreads*. Goodreads Inc. http://www.goodreads.com/author/quotes/103931 7.Dieter_F_Uchtdorf

71. Omartian, Stormie. *Power of a Praying Woman*. Harvest House, 2002.

About the Author

AJ Silva has served in various ministries in the Church of the Nazarene for over 16 years. He is ordained as an Elder in the Church of the Nazarene, and he currently serves as Lead Pastor at Oakdale Family Church of the Nazarene in Oakdale, CA. AJ attended Olivet Nazarene University, received a Bachelor of Arts in Pastoral Ministries from the Nazarene Bible College, and received a Master of Divinity from Regent University. He also has a heart for the military, which has led him to serve for five years with the Chaplain Corps as a Religious Program Specialist for the US Navy, providing religious support and physical security for chaplains.

Silva has been married to his wonderful and supportive wife, Hope, for the past nine years. They are blessed with two children, Melissa Ann and Thatcher Bryan.

You can follow AJ Silva's online blog by visiting http://pastoraj.weebly.com/ or follow his podcast "Understanding Misunderstandings: Lies We Don't Even Know We Believe" by going to http://understandingmisunderstandings.podbean.com/.

About Sermon To Book

SermonToBook.com began with a simple belief: that sermons should be touching lives, *not* collecting dust. That's why we turn sermons into high-quality books that are accessible to people all over the globe.

Turning your sermon series into a book exposes more people to God's Word, better equips you for counseling, accelerates future sermon prep, adds credibility to your ministry, and even helps make ends meet during tight times.

John 21:25 tells us that the world itself couldn't contain the books that would be written about the work of Jesus Christ. Our mission is to try anyway. Because, in heaven, there will no longer be a need for sermons or books. Our time is now.

If God so leads you, we'd love to work with you on your sermon or sermon series.

Visit www.sermontobook.com to learn more.

49676624R00074

Made in the USA
San Bernardino, CA
01 June 2017